Reading
Biblical Narratives

Reading
Biblical Narratives

Literary Criticism
and the
Hebrew Bible

Yairah Amit

Fortress Press
Minneapolis

READING BIBLICAL NARRATIVES
Literary Criticism and the Hebrew Bible

Translated from Hebrew by Yael Lotan

Cover art: The pastel painting of Rebekah is titled "And the damsel was very fair to look upon. . . . And she went down to the well and filled her pitcher, and went up" (Gen 24:16), ca. 1955, by the Israeli artist Abel Pann (1883–1963). Used by permission of the Mayanot Gallery, Jerusalem, Israel. We gratefully acknowledge the kind permission and courtesy of Itiel Pann, son of the artist.

Frontispiece: King David playing the lyre, floor mosaic, synagogue in Gaza, 6th century C.E. Collection of the Israel Antiquities Authority. Photo © The Israel Museum, Jerusalem. Used by permission.

Cover and book design: Zan Ceeley

Library of Congress Cataloging-in-Publication Data
Amit, Yairah.
    Reading biblical narratives : literary criticism and the Hebrew Bible /
    Yairah Amit.
        p. cm.
    Includes bibliographical references and index.
    ISBN 0-8006-3280-x (alk. paper)
     1. Bible. O.T.—Criticism, Narrative. 2. Narration in the Bible.
    3. Hebrew language—Style. 4. Bible as literature. I. Title.

    BS1182.3 .A45 2001
    221.6'6—dc21

                                        00-066259

Manufactured in the U.S.A.   AF 1-3280
05   04   03   02   01   1   2   3   4   5   6   7   8   9   10

To the Wonderful Four—my children
Yariv, Efrat, Helit, and Yoav

In the hope that they will
"in turn tell their children. . . ."

Contents

Preface

THE DRIVING QUESTIONS IN THIS WORK ARE: How does the Bible itself regard its narrative portions? Do biblical stories share peculiar characteristics, and can we speak about the particular nature of the biblical story? Who set the boundaries of these stories, and who was responsible for their headings? Should a reader of these stories bear in mind the considerations of biblical criticism and the findings of biblical research? Who is the omniscient and omnipotent figure in biblical narrative, God or the narrator? How are the plot, characters, time, and place designed? What is the relationship between content and form? How can we determine the meaning of a story, and can it have more than one meaning? These issues, and others I have not listed, underlie the chapters of this book.

My aim is for this book to serve as an introduction to biblical narrative. Moreover, it is constructed in widening circles—from the decision of where to draw the boundaries of the story and how to examine the text from a critical viewpoint, through a discussion of its component parts, to the understanding of its intrinsic and contextual meanings. This method of reading progressively is achieved by looking at the same stories from different viewpoints.

Since the book was designed not only for academic readers but also for the nonspecialist, the accompanying notes are not meant to encompass the full academic discussion of any of the issues. Their purpose is to enable readers who wish to know more to use the bibliography and the notes as a key to further research.

Like its predecessor, *History and Ideology in the Bible: An Introduction to Historiography in the Hebrew Bible,* this book is an expanded adaptation of thirteen lectures delivered on the Israeli Broadcast University of Galei Tzahal (IDF radio station) and Tel Aviv University in the winter of 1999–2000. The lectures were intended to serve as an introduction to the world of biblical narrative, and the same is true of this book.

While reading, it is advisable to keep a copy of the Bible at hand and to look up the stories as they are discussed. In this way, readers may refresh their memory of them and take note of the particular features being treated. The Bible translation I have used is the *Tanakh: The New Jewish Publication Society Translation according to the Traditional Hebrew Text* (1988), also called NJPS.

Sadly, Tirza Yuval, who helped shape the lectures from start to finish with her excellent guidance and editorial skill, died a short time after the original Hebrew edition was published. It is my pleasure to thank Jan Willem van Henten and Athalya Brenner, who provided me with wonderful working conditions during the summer of 1999, and in whose pleasant company the lectures were written. Great thanks to Ed Silver from the University of Chicago, who devoted time and goodwill putting some final touches on this book. Many thanks are due to my friend Ed Greenstein, who once again took the trouble to go over the manuscript prior to publication. However, the responsibility for its final form is my own. And last but not least to Yael Lotan, who translated it into English.

One

The Power of Stories

A CONSIDERABLE PART OF BIBLICAL LITERATURE consists of stories. Those who love measurements tell us that stories occupy fully one-third of the Bible. These stories tell us about humanity's early days, the place of Israel among the ancient Near Eastern peoples, and the history of the link between God and God's people, from the days of the patriarchs to the fall of Jerusalem and the return to Zion, and a great deal more.

The Bible makes plain that it ascribes great importance to stories and their presentation as a means of persuasion. The Bible even includes stories in which one person succeeds in persuading another by means of a story. Such is the case for Judah, who must persuade his brother Joseph not to harm Benjamin, the youngest of his brothers. To do this, he tells Joseph, who is at this time the viceroy of Pharaoh, King of Egypt, the full story of his family. Indeed, after hearing this moving and effective tale, Joseph cannot hide his emotion any longer; he breaks down and reveals his identity to his brothers (Gen 44:18—45:2).

In another example, when the prophet Nathan wants to reproach King David for the sin of seducing Bathsheba and causing the death of her husband, Uriah the Hittite, he tells him the story about the poor man's ewe lamb, which turns out to be a parable (2 Sam 12:1-14). David listens to the story, sympathizes with the poor man whose only lamb has been taken away from him, blames the rich man, and even condemns him to death. At this point Nathan draws the analogy between the rich man and David and makes him acknowledge his guilt.

A third example is also connected to the era of David. Joab, the captain of King David's army, seeing that David is longing for his son Absalom, who has fled to the land of Geshur after having Amnon killed, tries to persuade him to bring Absalom back. He summons a "clever woman" from the city of Tekoa, who tells the king what appears to be her own personal story (2 Sam 13:38—14:24). She talks about her widowhood, about a fight between her two sons, one of whom killed the other, about the family's determination to kill the survivor, and of her fear that the family's name will be extinguished when the last son is gone. When David promises her his support, she ties her story to the case of Absalom, and then David agrees to bring him back from the land of Geshur.

These three examples show that a story itself can be a means of persuasion and tell us much about its rhetorical functions in the biblical world. Since biblical literature sought to convince its audience (readers or listeners), the device of stories was employed.[1] It seems reasonable to assume that the authors of biblical narratives believed that if they told their flock about God's mighty deeds—how God saved the people in times of distress, how their fate was in God's hands, and how it paid to obey God—then the community of worshipers would keep its side of the covenant and remain faithful to God. Much depended on the power of stories, because a good story is irresistibly persuasive. Given its impact on its audience and the intention to influence them to accept its views, it is no wonder, then, that biblical literature abounds in stories.[2]

The stories have reached us in written form, but most biblical scholars are convinced—though there is no solid evidence—that, at least in part, they were transmitted orally for generations, as epics or legends (heroic tales of a local or national character), before being written down.[3] Once written down, the intention was not to while away long evenings in a world without electricity, movies, and television but to educate the readers or listeners and to persuade them to cling to the covenant and obey God's precepts. There is no mistaking the purpose of putting these stories in writing—it was to secure their preservation for as long as possible and to try to ensure that they reflected their authors' aims.[4] In this sense, they compare unfavorably with oral traditions, which usually keep mutating so that at times the story as told bears little resemblance to the original. Oral narrators pour something of their own personalities into the stories and may even adapt them to a given audience. As a result, there may be little resemblance between two tellings of a single story to different audiences. The story changes from telling to telling and from storyteller to storyteller.[5]

The process of writing down these stories also called for a change of form, as required by the new situation of narration that offers itself in reading. Oral stories, for example, are characterized by repetitions, fixed verbal formulas, even a fixed set of motifs typified by familiar scenes, such as a meeting at a well, a description of a journey or an annunciation, and so forth.[6] Such repetitions make things easier for the storyteller as well as for the audience. The storyteller knows that the listeners may lose concentration or miss a detail. Since neither the storyteller nor the listeners can turn back a page, repetitions are inserted that serve as reminders, which enable the listeners to return to the narrative and to remain attentive. These repetitions also enable the late arrival to pick up the thread of the narrative and join the rest of the audience and allow all the listeners to take part in the act of telling. The storyteller is thereby freed from the need constantly to astonish the audience with new motifs. This phenomenon of repetition is known to us both from classical epics, such as the *Iliad* and the *Odyssey*, and from cultures in which epics are still transmitted orally. These epics reveal the tendency of oral narrators to extend the story and often to tell it in meter, which makes it easier to participate and to remember.

The writer of stories must employ different techniques appropriate to the situation and to a more sophisticated, literate audience. When the writer does use repetition, it can be more complicated and varied, demanding closer attention and sometimes even close reading.[7] The writer knows that at least some of the audience are educated and capable of comparing texts and may expect a more sophisticated reading experience.

The reduced use of repetitions and the use of stories that were not necessarily recited caused biblical writers to produce shorter texts. Furthermore, writing short stories calls for literary techniques with special functions, so that a concise, even minimal delivery will still convey the story in an interesting and convincing way, thus serving its intended purpose.

An examination of three versions of one very short tale shows the distinctive quality of the biblical narrative. When you have read the three versions that follow, all taken from ancient sources, try to determine which one is biblical and what qualities make it so.

The story I have chosen for this purpose describes Samson's visit to a whore in Gaza and his heroic exploit of uprooting and carrying away the gates of the city.

Version one

> After this combat Samson, scorning the Philistines, came to Gaza and lodged at one of the inns. Thereupon the chiefs of the Gazites, informed of his presence in the town, posted ambuscades before the gates, to prevent his leaving it without their knowledge. But Samson, not unaware of these

schemes, when midnight was come, arose, flung himself against the gates, hoisted them—posts, bolts, woodwork and all—upon his shoulders, bore them to the mountain above Hebron and there deposited them.

Version two

And afterwards Samson was angry at [Gaza], and they locked him up and surrounded the city, and said, "Behold now our enemy has been delivered into our hands, and now let us gather together and let us save our own lives." And when Samson arose at night and saw the city locked up, he said, "Behold now those fleas have locked me up in their own city, and now the Lord will be with me, and I will go through their gates and attack them." And he came and put his left hand beneath the bar of the gate, and he took down the gate from the wall by shaking it. One part of it he kept in his right hand for a shield; the other he put on his shoulders. And he carried it because he had no sword, and he pursued the Philistines with it and killed 25,000 men with it. And he took up everything that made up the gate and brought them up to the mountain.

Version three

Once Samson went to Gaza; there he met a whore and slept with her. The Gazites [learned] that Samson had come there, so they gathered and lay in ambush for him in the town gate the whole night; and all night long they kept whispering to each other, "When daylight comes we'll kill him." But Samson lay in bed only till midnight. At midnight he got up, grasped the doors of the town gate with the two gateposts, and pulled them out along with the bar. He placed them on his shoulders and carried them off to the top of the hill that is near Hebron.

It seems that there is no mistaking the biblical quality of the third version. However, before discussing it, let us see what does not comport with biblical poetics in the first two versions.

The language of the first version is obviously not biblical, either in vocabulary, in the way words are formed, or in syntax. The author, Josephus, a historian of the first century c.e., included this passage in his book *Jewish Antiquities,* originally written in Greek for a Roman-Hellenistic audience (*Ant.* 5.304–5). He naturally used words that were familiar to his readers but strange to the biblical ear: for example, "inns,"[8] or "the chiefs of the Gazites."[9] He also avoided the distinctive biblical syntax with its typical *waw consecutive* structure (*wayyo'mer, wayyelek,* etc.) and used the appropriate Greek narrative syntax.

The author of the second version is known as Pseudo-Philo, because his writing was erroneously attributed to Philo of Alexandria, a Jewish philosopher who lived in Egypt in the first century c.e. It is now commonly accepted that this is an anonymous composition from around 100 c.e. (Harrington 1985:299).[10] The scholarly world was introduced to this book in late Latin manuscripts, but in 1898 scholars became convinced that the "Latin text is a translation from the Greek and that underlying the Greek there must have been a Hebrew original" (Harrington 1985:298–99). As the original language is only hypothesized, in this case I shall focus on the content (Harrington 1985:356–57).

In this version (43:1-3) Samson refers to the Philistines as "fleas" and expects God to be with him. This depiction contradicts the spirit of the biblical narrative, since if the Philistines were mere "fleas," there would be no need to call for God's help. The description here is also too detailed and does not accord with the biblical preference for brevity. Samson's exploit of uprooting the gates is told in minute detail, described in a series of verbs (see v. 3): *came, put, took down by shaking, kept, put, carried, pursued, killed.* We are told exactly what he did with each hand. Moreover, we get an added explanation about how the gates served both as a shield and as a weapon for killing 25,000 Philistines. Yet this prolix description does not even suggest where Samson carried the gates, and the absence of a geographical point too is uncharacteristic of biblical writing. Finally, it seems that this author was too pious to associate Samson with either inns or whores. Pseudo-Philo's Samson was simply angry with the city of Gaza.[11]

In contrast to the versions above, the biblical narrative (Judg 16:1-3) is concise and characterized by its own distinctive qualities. Here I am not referring to syntax and vocabulary[12] but to the following features:

The biblical narrative is never pious or coy. It does not flinch from the human aspect and has no difficulty describing Samson, the Danite hero, visiting a whore, just as it does not recoil from describing how the spies sent by Joshua went to the house of the harlot Rahab, a good place for picking up the local gossip (Joshua 2). Only later pious commentators described her as a seller of provisions.[13]

The biblical story makes skillful use of repetition. The experienced reader will immediately spot the repetition of the word "night," which occurs four times in this extremely short story: twice in order to emphasize the whole long night and twice to point out a specific time ("midnight")—"they gathered and lay in ambush for him in the town gate the *whole night;* and *all night long* they kept whispering. . . . But Samson lay in bed only till *midnight.* At *midnight* he got up . . ." (Judg 16:2-3, italics added). Assuming that repetitions are never accidental but always purposeful, we may look more closely and see that they serve to underline the impressive exploit (actually a miracle) and also sharpen the mockery of the Philistines and the satiric depiction of this exploit. The Philistines "kept whispering to each other" all night long, planning to capture and kill Samson, while he slipped out of the city at midnight right under their noses. This means that they were still plotting away in whispers when he was already gone with their city gate on his shoulders. Moreover, he must have performed this presumably noisy exploit—tearing out the city gate, complete with gateposts and bar—extremely quietly. Needless to say, the gate of an ancient walled city had to be a massive object. Thus we see how the author's irony and mockery of the Philistines are implicit in the story. The reader is directed to infer it by the repeated use of the word "night."[14]

In addition, let us note the careful description of this miraculous deed. The phrase "the spirit of the LORD gripped him" recurs several times in the stories about Samson in Judges—as when he tears the lion apart, "as one might tear a kid asunder" (14:6); when he kills thirty men of Ashkelon and stripped them (14:19); and when he breaks his bonds and kills a thousand men with the jawbone of an ass (15:14-15). Yet in this story, as in the stories of the bees (14:8-9), the foxes (15:3-5), and of what happens in Delilah's bedchamber (16:6-14), there is no mention of the spirit of the Lord. In other words, not every act of strength merits such a mention, even though it is understood that only God's will and spirit makes it possible. The spirit of the Lord is highly revered and is mentioned only in awe-inspiring events, not in less respectable contexts, such as those involving insects, foxes, a visit to a whore, and the negotiations in Delilah's bedroom.[15]

Emphasizing God's spirit in the event makes it seem improbable, since miracles, by definition, are extraordinary. Yet the biblical stories are meant to appear as historical events that really occurred. That is why the storyteller took pains to define the locale. This particular story begins in Gaza and ends on "the top of the hill that is near Hebron." Josephus, as a historian, also mentions Hebron, whereas Pseudo-Philo does not. Indeed, by defining the area in question, the exploit becomes even more impressive: Samson carries the gates of the city on his back a long way uphill, some forty miles, starting on the coast and ending on top of a hill overlooking Hebron, impressing the reader even more by the scope of the deed.

The examination of this exceptionally brief biblical story—a mere three verses long—and the comparison with the way it is told in the other versions reveals its distinctive rules and characteristic narrative style. In designing the story, the author considered different issues, such as when and how to refer to God, when and against whom to deploy the weapon of irony and mockery, and whether it is permissible to describe a biblical hero, chosen and sent forth by God, as a creature of desires, passions, and weaknesses. The author also planned how to keep the story short, and at what cost, as well as other considerations and stylistic devices, which will be discussed in later chapters. Frank Polak's introduction to his book *The Biblical Narrative* illustrates these points:

> The stories of the Bible are part of the foundation of culture, art and literature. These stories have been transmitted by generations of Jews and Christians—some of them also by Muslims—and have proved an inexhaustible source of inspiration to painters, writers and composers, showing their capacity to move their readers. Nevertheless, it is not easy to define the artistic nature of these stories: they bear no resemblance to a modern story, in their style, in the plot structure and in characterization. The extent of the biblical story is much narrower than the modern reader is accustomed to. The elements of its design are concentrated in a relatively small scope, and utilize this smallness to achieve great power and tension. Therefore, what is considered appropriate from the story's viewpoint is not necessarily what appeals to us, and what we take for granted does not always appeal to the biblical narrator. Thus, to examine these stories you must study their particular qualities. (1994:ix)

Two

Story Scholars and the Role of the Reader

HAVING RECOGNIZED THAT THE BIBLICAL STORY follows rules of its own—meaning that it is distinguished by particular literary qualities—we move on to the next question: When did biblical studies start to treat the biblical story as a discrete subject of research? In other words, when did scholars begin to study and analyze the literary techniques developed by the authors of biblical stories?

Research on Biblical Narrative

The treatment of biblical narrative as an independent genre and a subject of poetic analysis is a relatively new addition to biblical research. In all, the systematic, critical study of the Bible is a recent area of research in the last two hundred years, pioneered by scholars in the fields of history and philology. They applied research methods taken from the study of classical literature with the central purpose of uncovering the seeds of historical truth, so as to reconstruct the history of the Israelites and their culture.[1] The issues of chief concern for these scholars were: Who wrote what and when? That is, what is the history of the text, the stages of the composition and its writing, and the historical circumstances in which it was written, which are possibly more strongly reflected than the period described? This deliberately historical approach inevitably meant ignoring the aesthetic aspects of the text. Scholars were not unaware of problems of form and aesthetic features, but these were marginalized or even used as evidence of inconsistencies in the text. While some of the Sages, the Church Fathers, and the medieval and traditional Jewish commentators were aware of such features as style, meaning, characters, sequence, and so forth, they too, like the critical scholars, did not pursue these issues systematically or for their own sake.[2]

The first call to examine the artistic aspects of the sagas of the Book of Genesis was made by the German scholar Hermann Gunkel early in the twentieth century (Gunkel 1997). But Gunkel confined this call to the introduction of his commentary on Genesis, while the body of the book continued in the historical-philological trend.[3] His students developed the analysis of literary forms by sorting the stories into subgroups and searching for common elements of form that would serve to categorize them; for example, etiological stories, cult legends, annunciation stories, and others (Tucker 1971; Hayes 1974).

Franz Rosenzweig and Martin Buber pioneered the focus on poetics and its relation to meaning in biblical studies in the 1920s and 1930s. Rosenzweig devoted an article to "The Secret of Biblical Narrative Form" (1994), and Buber concentrated on specific stylistic features, such as the "leading word" (1994a, 1994b).[4] Although these scholars noted the close association between content and form, their work still lacked a comprehensive view of the biblical story and did not deal with the subject systematically.

The turning point that launched a systematic analysis of the formal aspect of biblical literature by applying the lessons of the new science of literature—such as the "Werkinterpretation" of central Europe and the Anglo-Saxon "New Criticism"—appeared in Meir Weiss's methodological work, *The Bible from Within: The Method of Total Interpretation*, published in Hebrew in 1962.[5] Though his discussion and examples dealt mainly with biblical poetry rather than narrative, at that time he also published an article in the journal *Molad* entitled "The Poetics of Biblical Narrative: Researching the Biblical Narrative according to the Latest Methods of Literary Criticism" (Weiss 1963a).[6] His work and that of others who were influential in the late 1950s and the early 1960s were followed by a series of articles and books by other scholars, who also concentrated on the story.[7] Weiss's method, which he called "total interpretation," is a literary synchronic approach, as opposed to the dominant historical diachronic one, which means it ignores the history of the text and its stratification, and concentrates on the story's meaning in relation to its formal design.

The synchronic approach, which examines the story as we find it and pays no attention to its history, was given a strong boost in an innovative and provocative article by Menahem Perry and Meir Sternberg: "The King through Ironic Eyes: The Narrator's Devices in the Biblical Story of David and Bathsheba and Two Excurses on the Theory of Narrative Text" (1968), which appeared in the periodical *Hasifrut* (*Literature*).[8] It set off a lively and productive argument among biblical scholars and was warmly welcomed by literary scholars. It concluded with the following words:

> It might be asked, how do we justify such a reading of a "primitive" story, written by a "naive" author in an ancient period, of whose "literary theory" we know nothing? Does it make sense to analyze a biblical text as though it were written by Nabokov or Agnon? To which we would reply that this story, just like any other, be it modern or classical, must be given the most complex and organized interpreta-

tion, linking together the maximum amount of facts (details, tones, subtleties) in the richest, most complete and logical manner, with constant attention to the text and its tendencies as they unfold with it.

Thus the proof of the correctness of our approach to this story is entirely practical: reading with close attention to details and subtleties, presupposing the existence of the text's semantic substance, "pays off" better than any other kind of reading, because it delivers the story in the richest, clearest, most complex, complete and organized manner.

The age of the text makes no difference. It is from the story of David and Bathsheba itself that we infer its poetics, just as we do with Lolita, regardless of what its author or the modern theory of literature may say. (292)[9]

Since the publication of Perry and Sternberg's article, there have been many studies, articles, and books that share the following assumption: Even if we cannot regard the biblical story as a separate genre, the art of the biblical story is, in the words of the literary scholar Robert Alter, a "wonderfully complex art," which "offers such splendid illustrations of the primary possibilities of narrative" (1981:x; see also 3–22). Moreover, since the biblical stories are ancient literature incorporated into a collection of works written over a period of at least six hundred years (from the eighth to the second century B.C.E.), we modern readers must learn to identify the principles that informed their design.[10] This, then, is a young and novel area of study, less than fifty years old, that analyzes biblical texts as literary works and deserves to be studied and tested according to the criteria of literary criticism.[11] The value of this scholarship and its contribution to biblical research is no longer in doubt. Tradition-minded readers enjoy discovering an added aspect of these stories, namely, the aesthetic one, while the historian who seeks to reconstruct the realities behind the narrative finds that in order to elucidate the historical core, it is necessary to observe the formal design.[12] The last three

decades have seen a number of new literary methods being applied
to the biblical story, representing a variety of reading strategies, such
as structuralist, poststructuralist, feminist, and deconstructionist;
and there are probably more to come.

On the Role of the Reader

Before we begin to trace the principles discovered while studying
the biblical stories, we must tackle one basic question: Who determines the boundaries of a story—or, in other words, who is
responsible for determining that a story begins and ends at certain
points?

A casual reader of biblical literature who ignores the chapter
divisions of the Bible, which date from the beginning of the thir-
teenth century, discovers that there are narrative sequences that do
not correspond to the outlines of the stories.[13] For example, sometimes a chapter contains several stories, and sometimes a story
goes beyond the chapter boundary. Thus, the story of creation
begins in chapter 1 of the Book of Genesis and ends in chapter 2,
with the depiction of God resting on the seventh day. Most scholars consider that this story ends in the middle of verse 4.[14] On
the other hand, Judges 16 includes three stories: Samson and
the Gazite whore (vv. 1-3), Samson and Delilah (vv. 4-21), and
finally the death of Samson in the temple of Dagon (vv. 22-31a).[15]
These boundaries are not a formal division imposed upon the
reader, who may disagree with it. In this particular case, these divisions are widely accepted by commentators, though not all of
them. In any event, before discussing any one biblical story, we
must determine its boundaries.

Before we launch into the story itself, we ought to consider
how a particular sequence of verses represents a story by tackling
the problem of boundaries. An excellent illustration of this prob-

lem was the debate that followed Perry and Sternberg's article mentioned above (1968). Perry and Sternberg confined their discussion of the story of David and Bathsheba to 2 Samuel 11, which deals with the sin, while their critics, Boaz Arpali (1970) and Uriel Simon (1970), argued that these set limits were misleading. They criticized what they regarded as an arbitrary separation between chapter 11, which describes the sin of David, from its sequel in chapter 12, which deals with the encounter between David and Nathan, including the parable of the poor man's ewe-lamb, Nathan's admonition, and his description of the retribution to be meted to David and his house. In other words, Arpali and Simon maintained that it was a mistake to analyze chapter 11 by itself, and that the story's true unit was chapters 11 and 12 (2 Sam 11:1—12:31), which, as a whole, was not ironic so much as a moral chastisement.

Without going into the details of that stimulating debate, I should note that its great contribution was to bring the issue of the boundaries of stories into discussion. Perry and Sternberg, in their response article, "Caution: A Literary Text! Problems in the Poetics and Interpretation of Biblical Narrative," showed that the problem of demarcating a literary unit as an object of research was not exclusive to the biblical sphere but could arise in the analysis of any literary work.[16] A given unit may be regarded as whole in relation to smaller units and as a part in relation to larger ones—in the same way that an act in a play may be regarded as a whole unit in relation to the scenes that comprise it and as a part of the whole play. The question then arises if the commentator may choose to deal with either a particular scene or a whole act as the object of his research. Here is how Perry and Sternberg responded:

> The boundaries of a unit are dynamic; they are not defined in advance, once and for all, but are redefined and reorganized anew, according to the questions one seeks to answer, according to the kind of observation that one wishes to

> apply. . . . Every researcher and every research demarcate their own boundaries, and are quite free to do so, provided they take into account—explicitly or implicitly—all the other frameworks, both narrower and wider, to which the unit in question belongs. (1970:632)

Such a dynamic view of unit boundaries is especially appropriate to the analysis of biblical stories. Since we find them today as parts in a sequence of events, we have no way of knowing what boundaries their authors or editors had in mind.

The story of Joseph, which begins in Genesis 37 and continues to the end of the book (chap. 50), illustrates this approach. The reader or commentator may choose to look at the whole story, or particular units within it, such as Joseph in the house of Potiphar and his wife (chap. 39), or the dreams of the cupbearer and the baker (chap. 40). In choosing such a unit, one must define its beginning and end. Or, if one were to choose the motif of dreams in the whole story, one would pick out all six dreams that appear in the course of it: Joseph's two dreams (37:5-10), the dreams of the two courtiers (chap. 40), and Pharaoh's two dreams (41:1-38). This means the reader or commentator must decide where to draw the outlines of the chosen narrative unit.

Biblical stories have no original titles, and indeed the familiar titles—for example, the binding of Isaac, the story of creation, the story of the flood—are products of exegetical tradition, which assigned titles to fit the contents of the stories. As a result, the title of any biblical story is a product of a commentator, and the reader is free to disagree with it and to change it. That is to say, the reader may engage in the same work as the various commentators who gave different titles to the same story. What all this means is that the biblical stories call for dynamic reading, which must determine the boundaries of the stories and even their titles. As you examine the various commentaries, you will come across different outlines and titles since the boundaries and titles are not holy writ but the reader's determination.

We may then ask if any particular demarcation is based on some specific criterion or is entirely arbitrary. The debate about the outlines of the story of David and Bathsheba shows that both sides—Perry and Sternberg, and Arpali and Simon—were in fact applying similar criteria or yardsticks. For example, both think that the thematic aspect must be taken into consideration. Arpali argues that the story of David and Bathsheba was a tale of sin and punishment, as inextricable elements, and therefore chapters 11 and 12 have to be considered as one unit. Perry and Sternberg, on the other hand, maintain that it is possible to separate the sin from the punishment and analyze each stage by itself.[17]

In the case of the concubine in Gibeah, which begins in Judges 19 and finishes at the end of chapter 21, any reader would separate chapter 19 from chapter 20. The first chapter relates the story of the sin of the town of Gibeah and describes the circumstances of the rape of the concubine, while the second describes the war waged by the tribes of Israel against Benjamin and tells the story of the punishment for that sin. Sometimes sin and punishment are bound up in a single story, such as the sin of Adam and Eve and their expulsion from the Garden of Eden; at other times sin and punishment appear as two clearly definable stories. Sometimes, too, there is a story of a sin that remains without punishment, as in the story of the northward journey of the tribe of Dan, who conquered the city of Laish and set up a shrine there (Judges 17–18). Here the Danites are depicted as a band of outlaws who robbed and looted Micah's shrine, conquered a peaceable city, and established a shrine with a divine image in it. In this story, whose purpose is to illustrate the statement that "in those days there was no king in Israel; everyone did as he pleased" (Judg 17:6; 18:1a), the Danites are not punished—proving that punishment did not always follow sin.[18]

The debate between Perry and Sternberg and their critics Arpali and Simon brought out a number of criteria, none of which is absolute. Taken together, they can guide readers of biblical literature in demarcating any units. In addition to the thematic criterion, they proposed a structural one, a principle of symmetry (or inclusio), that is, beginning and ending with a similar subject, phrase, or word. Another criterion pertains to considerations of time—relating to events that happened in one period of time. Finally, there are considerations of poetics and of style, such as techniques of narration that characterize a specific unit; for example, ironic representation, use of key words, and the like (Perry and Sternberg 1970:637–38).

The application of these criteria can be simple enough. For example, in the story of creation (Gen 1:1—2:4a) there is no question that the subject is the creation of the world by God in seven days. The concentric quality too is obvious: the unit opens and closes with similar statements: "When God began to create heaven and earth . . ." (Gen 1:1) and "Such is the story of heaven and earth when they were created" (Gen 2:4a). It encompasses a definable unit of time: creation in seven days. The unit is also characterized by a distinctive style: detailed and dry, with repetitive formulas, such as "And it was so," and "And there was evening and there was morning, such-and-such a day."

Following Perry and Sternberg and applying these criteria to the story of the sin of David and Bathsheba (2 Samuel 11) reveals that it is legitimate to view it as a definable unit, and that its separation from chapter 12 is not arbitrary. Chapter 11 focuses on the sin, and it begins and ends with Bathsheba being brought to the king's house (2 Sam 11:4, 27a), so that the motif of her passage to the palace is also the time frame of her passage through pregnancy. It is also characterized by a distinctive style, containing a touch of irony and implied criticism of the king (except for the final words, v. 27b), which contrast with the direct reproving tone of the following story of the punishment (2 Samuel 12). Yet the same criteria may also be applied to the unit consisting of chapters 11–12: chapter 11 opens with the war against the Ammonites, and chapter 12 concludes with its outcome (the criterion of concentric structure). The event occurs in the king's house during the war (the criterion of time). It is an event of sin and punishment (the criterion of theme), and as Simon and Arpali showed, the two chapters share common features of language and motifs.[19]

Thus, we have two legitimate options, depending on the defined subject: the examination of the story of sin and punishment and an analysis of the wider unit, comprising chapters 11 and 12; or an examination of the ironic view of the king, defining the subject as the king's sin, and focusing only on chapter 11.

We see that the first stage in determining the outline of the story is made by the reader or commentator who defines the subject, then examines it and refines it by applying the other criteria so as to avoid arbitrary points of separation. Here an additional criterion may be added, that of editorial phrases, such as "And it came to pass at that time" (NJPS: "At that time") or "And it came to pass after these things" (NJPS: "Some time afterwards," "some time later"; Gen 21:22; 22:1, 20). These and similar phrases are the editor's indication that here begins a new subject that is related to the preceding sequence, so that in many cases they indicate the beginning of a new story.

In the same way, the reader who examines the story of Samson and the Gazite whore will study the three verses in Judges 16 and soon will find that the other criteria may be applied even to this very brief unit. These other criteria are the concentric aspect (he came to Gaza and he left Gaza); time (apparently less than a whole day); and poetics and style (an ironic representation of the Philistines and a miracle story in which God is not mentioned). In this case we can also note the editorial phrase, "After that," which opens the story of Samson and Delilah (Judg 16:4) and thus indicates the end of the previous story. This phrase signals the end of the story about Samson and the Gazite whore, and the beginning of a new episode in Samson's life. Note that one more editorial phrase, characterizing the Book of Judges, "And he judged Israel" (Judg 15:20 [NJPS: "He led Israel"]), precedes the story about

Samson and the Gazite whore. Thus, the demarcation of this story, being placed between two editorial phrases and to which it is possible to apply the other criteria for delimiting textual boundaries, does not give rise to disagreements. To examine the subject of Samson and women, one must define a wider unit, beginning with Samson's marriage in chapter 14 and ending with Delilah delivering him into the hands of the Philistines (Judg 16:21). To examine the life of Samson, one must consider all the stories about him, specifically, the whole circle of Samson stories (Judges 13–16).

Similarly, a reader who wishes to concentrate on the birth of Samuel alone will select 1 Sam 1:1-20, which concludes with his birth and the meaning of his name: "Hannah conceived, and at the turn of the year bore a son. She named him Samuel, meaning, 'I asked the LORD for him.'" A reader who wishes to examine Hannah's vow and its reward will go on reading beyond the end of the chapter (v. 28), when she leaves her son at the shrine, to 2:11a, where the story closes in a concentric manner with the return from Shiloh to the family home in Ramah: "Then Elkanah [and Hannah] went home to Ramah."[20] Uriel Simon, for example, stresses the double giving—the human and the divine: Hannah's vow and her reward—and adds to that unit the verses that state that Hannah later had more sons and daughters (1 Sam 2:18-21a).[21]

These examples show to what extent the demarcation of the unit depends on the selection and definition of the subject. We might even say that the titles and boundaries are interdependent. The following titles show how each one refers to a unit of different scope: "The Sin of Adam and Eve in the Garden of Eden," "Sin and Punishment in the Garden of Eden," and "The Story of the Garden of Eden." The third suggests the broadest scope, since it includes everything to do with the Garden of Eden, from its creation to the expulsion of Adam and Eve (Gen 2:4b—3:24). The title "Sin and Punishment in the Garden of Eden" refers to a smaller unit, consisting of the last verse of chapter 2 and the whole of chapter 3. This smaller unit states that Adam and Eve were naked yet they felt no shame, whereas when they were expelled they were dressed, having learned shame (Gen 2:25—3:24). The title "The Sin of Adam and Eve in the Garden of Eden" suggests the narrowest scope, referring to the single scene describing the enticement and the eating of the forbidden fruit (3:1-7). We see that the titles, chosen and defined by the reader, are the most important factor in determining the scope of the unit. At the same time, it is necessary to verify that a unit defined as a story does not violate most of the mentioned criteria, which are inclusio, time, language, and style, as well as editorial phrases, if any.

The above discussion has shown not only that the outline of the story is dynamically determined, but also that the reader of biblical stories has an unusually active role, in the absence of clear boundaries and titles.[22] The reader who defines the subject determines its scope.

Three

A Biblical Story
alongside Biblical Criticism

THE PREVIOUS CHAPTER OPENED with a description of the relatively new branch of Bible research that deals with biblical stories. This chapter focuses on the relationship between general Bible research with its critical conclusions and the study of biblical stories. Do story scholars adopt the conclusions of Bible criticism as their assumptions, do they consider them, or do they ignore them altogether?

A historical examination of this issue shows that all three possibilities can be found in the scholarship. The choice of a particular approach may reflect a scholar's background and training, ideological persuasion, and even psychological inclinations. Some scholars who, consciously or otherwise, regard the biblical text as sacred, even while treating it as an object of study, would not only prefer to ignore the critical conclusions of biblical research but would happily adopt those literary synchronic approaches that analyze the existing text without asking questions about its history. Other scholars may do so because this suits their theoretical outlook, which rests on principles that lead them to ignore the history of the text, or because they are unfamiliar with the results of historical biblical studies. On the other hand, those scholars who regard the biblical text as a subject of research like any other, and whose professional and critical outlook makes it impossible for them to ignore the historical (diachronic) dimension, seek to combine the two approaches.

Following the developments in research on classical literature, two kinds of approaches have developed in Bible criticism: literary criticism (or higher criticism) and textual criticism (or lower criticism). The purpose of these two approaches is to reconstruct, as much as possible, the putative original shape of the biblical text or to discover the pristine texts (Tov 1992:168). Textual criticism is concerned with the variant readings that appear in the different ancient versions, their reasons, and their circumstances. This criticism addresses problems of writing, such as script and spelling, problems of transcription, and problems of transmission through the ages. This kind of criticism assumes that in the course of transmission the text became corrupted with unintentional deviations and errors. Literary criticism, however, is based on text criticism and takes its conclusions into consideration. This criticism is concerned with the text as a whole, its unity, the time of its writing, questions about its author or authors, and the intentional changes that may be discovered in it. Literary criticism offers assumptions about the original scope of the text and the various deliberate additions that were inserted into it in the course of its editing, which reflect the needs of later readers.

Using both methods of criticism would have advantages but was exceptional. For example, in *The Life of Samson,* Yair Zakovitch brings together both approaches:

> Our study combines the method of the narrative with an awareness of the need for higher criticism. It has become obvious that nowadays poetical analysis and higher biblical criticism are going their separate ways in the research of

biblical narrative. Scholars are usually occupied with the characteristic features of the biblical story, such as repetition, the shaping of the element of time and the like, or with analyzing individual stories that do not necessarily raise the problems of higher criticism (or even ignoring those problems). (1982:15)[1]

Further on Zakovitch states that "in our critical reading of the story of the life of Samson we will also seek to set the text straight . . ." (15). Zakovitch thus applies both text criticism and higher criticism, while making extensive use of the tools of literary criticism.

In the late 1960s and early 1970s such questions of text criticism and higher criticism were often ignored in analyzing biblical stories, as shown by Perry and Sternberg's article, "The King through Ironic Eyes" (1968; in English in Sternberg 1985: 186–222), or Sternberg's methodological essay, "A Delicate Balance in the Story of the Rape of Dinah: The Biblical Story and the Rhetoric of the Literary Creation" (1973; in English, 1985: 445–81). Since then it has become increasingly rare for commentators to ignore totally these aspects of Bible criticism. Sometimes the study opens with a reference to the results of Bible criticism, and sometimes they are represented in the notes. One example is from the theoretical and applied study by Sternberg, *The Poetics of Biblical Narrative: Ideological Literature and the Drama of Reading.* Sternberg comes from the field of literary theory and refers to Bible criticism right from the start in the context of a fundamental discussion of "Discourse and Source" (1985:7–23). To illustrate his view that we cannot ignore the condition of the text itself, he refers to the especially corrupt verse that opens the description of Saul's reign: "Saul was . . . years old when he became king, and he reigned over Israel two years" (1 Sam 13:1), which is obviously unreasonable (Sternberg 1985:14).[2] On the other hand, when discussing higher criticism, which he calls "source-oriented inquiry," he states that since its interest focuses "on some object behind the text," he prefers to do without them: "Discourse-oriented analysis, on the other hand, sets out to understand not the realities behind the text but the text itself as a pattern of meaning and effect" (1985:15).

As one who takes an interest in all aspects of Bible criticism and who finds ways of applying them where necessary, while using the tools of literary criticism, I shall try to show that if it is possible, the first stage in analyzing a biblical story must be to obtain the information provided by Bible criticism about the particular text. This allows its evaluation at the stage of the literary analysis, with the tools of literary criticism. Let us begin with three examples concerning textual criticism.

First, the second sentence in the story of Samson and the Gazite harlot lacks something: "The Gazites [learned] that Samson had come there, so they gathered . . ." (Judg 16:2). It is unlikely that the writer preferred to ignore the verb "learned,"[3] and indeed most scholars assume that the verb simply dropped and complete the sentence according to the Septuagint.[4]

The second example is more complex and is from the story of Amnon and Tamar (2 Sam 13:1-22), in which Amnon, David's eldest son, raped his sister Tamar. The story concludes with the following narrator's statement: "When King David heard about all this, he was greatly upset. Absalom did not utter a word to Amnon, good or bad; but Absalom hated Amnon because he had violated his sister Tamar" (2 Sam 13:21-22). Here in the Masoretic Text, David, who hears and says nothing, appears passive. Checking this text against the complete Greek translation, the Septuagint, we find an additional verse that explains David's inaction: "but he did not grieve the spirit of his son Amnon, because he loved him, for he was his first-born" (1879:418). The complete Septuagint text shows how important this verse is in its context: "And King David heard of all these things, and was very angry; but he did *not* grieve the spirit of his son Amnon, because he loved him, for he was his first-born. And Abessalom spoke *not* to Amnon, good or bad, because Abessalom hated Amnon, on account of his humbling his sister Themar."[5] The reader of the Septuagint, which has a longer text, can easily understand why David said nothing because he valued primogeniture highly and had favorites in his relations with his children. Moreover, although as the king he was the supreme judge, he was unable to apply the principles of justice to his own household. Thus, not only David's role as the supreme judge is diminished in this version of the story but also his position as father and educator is criticized.

Significantly, we find that in another critical situation involving his sons, when Adonijah seeks to inherit his father's throne and thus prevent Solomon from becoming the next king, David displays a similar pattern of behavior: "Now Adonijah son of Hagith went about boasting, 'I will be king!' He provided himself with chariots and horses and an escort of fifty outrunners. His father had never scolded him, 'Why did you do that?' He was the one born after Absalom and, like him, was very handsome" (1 Kings 1:5-6, MT). This Masoretic Text not only shows David behaving in a similar way but explicitly refers to the previous story by mentioning Absalom and drawing the comparison: "and like him was very handsome." When we see the biblical author using allusions, we may conclude that he laid down an analogical basis for them. In other words, why not conclude that the plus verse in the Septuagint was original and was mistakenly left out of the Masoretic Text by a scribe's slip *(homoioteleuton)*. Attributing such allusions to the translator means viewing him as an author who sought not only to understand and even to explain the text but to improve deeply its poetics and aesthetics. A reader familiar with the Septuagint version of the story of Amnon and Tamar may well regard the extra verse as inseparable from the story, though it is missing in the Masoretic Text. Taking that version into account helps us to understand not only the personality of David, but also the relations between him and Absalom later on when he hears that the latter has taken the law into his own hands and murdered his brother Amnon, as well as his later rebellion against his father. Thus, the short sentence, "but he did not grieve the spirit of his son Amnon, because he loved him, for he was his first-born," which is preserved in the Septuagint and missing from the Masoretic Text, is not only a key to understanding the personalities and their conduct in the story of the rape but also sheds light on Absalom's motives when he murdered his brother and rebelled against his father. Needless to say, understanding the motives and perceiving them as justified gives the story added depth and mitigates David's attitude toward Absalom later on.

Just as the second example relates to characterization, the third example relates to plot. In the story about Hannah's fulfillment of her vow, after she has given birth to a son and weaned him, she brings three bulls to the shrine: "When she had weaned him, she took him up with her along with *three* bulls, *one* ephah of flour, and *a* jar of wine. And . . . brought him to the House of the LORD at Shiloh" (1 Sam 1:24, italics added). The text continues, "After slaughtering *the bull*, they brought the boy to Eli." The question arises, if the sacrifice was of one bull, why mention three bulls who have no place in the unfolding story? Since the work of Hermann Gunkel (1997:xxxix), we know that the biblical story, being very concise, retains only that which has some function in the plot. A disproportion also exists between one ephah of flour and one jar of wine versus three bulls. This discrepancy is puzzling, until we look into the Septuagint and discover that our text may be corrupted (see Tov 1992:253–54). There it says, "a calf of three years old"—recalling Abraham's covenant, when he sacrificed "a three-year-old heifer, a three-year-old she-goat, a three-year-old ram . . ." (Gen 15:9). We may therefore deduce that the Masoretic Text was corrupted by one scribe making an erroneous division of letters into words, so that a three-year-old bull (the Hebrew consonants, *pr mšlš*) became three bulls (*prm šlšh*), while another scribe made a different division. This kind of distortion resulted from the ancient stage of writing without separating the words, without vowels, and no special final letters. The last were put into the text only at a later stage. In analyzing the story, the Septuagint version that mentions one bull is less puzzling and fits well with the plot sequence.[6]

The above examples come from the sphere of text criticism and show its contribution to solving problems in the flow of the story. Let us now look at examples from the sphere of literary criticism.

After Gideon's triumph over the Midianites, he addressed his men as follows: "Each of you give me the earring he received as booty. . . . 'Certainly,' they replied and they spread out a cloth and everyone threw onto it the earring he had received as booty. The weight of the golden earrings he had requested came to 1,700 shekels of gold; this was in addition to the crescents, the pendants, and the purple robes worn by the kings of Midian, and in addition to the collars on the necks of their camels. Gideon made an ephod of this gold and set it up in his own town of Ophrah" (Judg 8:24-27a). In other words, Gideon collected the war booty and made it into a kind of victory monument. A similar way of commemorating a victory appears in the description of Moses' actions following the victory over the Amalekites. God said to Moses: "Inscribe this in a document as a reminder and read it aloud to Joshua: I will utterly blot out the memory of Amalek from under heaven! And Moses built an altar and named it Adonai-nissi" (Exod 17:14-15). Yet in Gideon's case, the making of the ephod is denounced: "There all Israel went astray after it, and it became a snare to Gideon and his household" (Judg 8:27b). Critical scholars regard this clause, which disapproves of Gideon's act, as a late insertion that did not exist in the original version and must therefore be left out in analyzing the meaning of the unit and the achievements of Gideon.[7]

Others maintain that it is necessary to analyze the unit as we find it, even though leaving it in makes for a difficult contradiction. If Gideon's act led to the Israelites becoming idolatrous, how can his career be viewed in a positive light, as suggested by the final verse in the chapter: "Nor did they show loyalty to the house of Jerubaal-Gideon in return for all the good that he had done for Israel" (Judg 8:35). How then are we to view Gideon: as one who did good, or as one who misled Israel and in effect did harm? Moreover, if Gideon was evil, then, according to the widespread biblical principle of collective reward, his sons deserve punishment and Abimelech who slaughtered all of Gideon's sons becomes a figure who carried out the retribution in accordance with God's will and the laws of divine justice. Yet at the end of the story of Abimelech the narrator states, "Thus God repaid Abimelech for the evil he had done to his father by slaying his seventy brothers . . ." (Judg 9:56-57; see also 9:23-24). The contradiction is obvious: Did Abimelech act on God's behalf, or did he do evil and had to be punished for it? The text before us is replete with inner contradictions, which run against the spirit of the Book of Judges as a whole, namely, the characterization of the judges as leaders who worshiped God and did not cause the people to do what was wrong in God's eyes. The problem of internal inconsistency disappears, however, if we accept the speculative argument of biblical criticism, that the description of Gideon as one who misled Israel is out of place, having been added by a later editor. Accordingly, Gideon did only good, whereas his son Abimelech was a bad character who did harm to his brothers and his people.

The question remains, why did that later editor describe Gideon as one who led the Israelites to idolatry? The answer I prefer is that this editor was a zealot, who came across the mention of the ephod, was uncertain as to its meaning, assumed it was a pagan image, and condemned Gideon. But, as this condemnation does not accord with the rest of the story, with regard to Gideon or Abimelech, we have to ask whether to regard such editing as part of the primary text. I am convinced we should not, and therefore, when analyzing the story of Gideon, I state in advance that the particular clause (8:27b) is probably a late addition, an editorial deviation resulting from broader contextual frameworks, and therefore should be put in brackets. At the same time, we should consider the fact that someone was interested in inserting it and ask who had such an interest, when, and why.

Our second example considers the familiar story of Naboth's vineyard (1 Kings 21). In this story Ahab, the king of Israel, covets the vineyard of Naboth the Jezreelite, which adjoins his palace, because he wants to enlarge his vegetable garden. Ahab offers Naboth another plot of land or a sum of money, but Naboth replies: "The LORD forbid that I should give up to you what I have inherited from my fathers!" (v. 3b). Ahab returns home glum and irritable, lays down on his bed, turns his face to the wall, and refuses to eat. Seeing this, his wife, Jezebel, promises to take care of the matter. She takes the king's seal and in his name writes a letter to the elders of Jezreel, telling them to accuse Naboth of reviling God and the king and to punish him with death. This is done, and Jezebel informs Ahab that the vineyard is his. When Ahab goes to the vineyard to take possession of it, he meets the prophet Elijah, who challenges him with the well-known phrase, "Would you murder and take possession?" (v. 19).

However, something strange happens in the text from the second half of verse 20 to the end of verse 26, which reports the rest of Elijah's speech. Instead of a direct, concrete challenge in the second person, concerning Naboth's vineyard, Elijah chastises Ahab for leading Israel into sin. Speaking of him in the third person, he declares that Ahab has strayed into idolatry at Jezebel's instigation, compares Ahab to other royal dynasties that preceded him and were destroyed, and finally describes him as the worst of all the kings of Israel. In addition, the entire passage is worded in the style typical of the deuteronomistic editor(s) of the Book of Kings, with none of the spontaneous discourse that characterizes the story to that point. Passages in that same style occur periodically in the Book of Kings, for example, the speech of Ahijah of Shiloh about Jeroboam son of Nabat, king of Israel (1 Kings 14: 7-11), or the speech of the prophet Jehu son of Hanani to Baasha, king of Israel (1 Kings 16:1-4, 13). Biblical scholars maintain that this passage is not an integral part of the original story but was interpolated at a later stage by the deuteronomistic editor of the Book of Kings.[8] Consequently, scholars who are aware of the difficulties caused by the presence of this passage, and who want to analyze the literary design of the story, declare in advance that they propose to ignore this passage. Other researchers, who concentrate on the editorial methods in the Book of Kings and the way in which the editor pieced together separate units into one whole book, examine this passage very carefully. If they ignore the arguments of Bible research, literary scholars will need to muster a number of reasons to explain why the prophet abruptly changes his style of speech, switches from the second- to the third-person singular, attacks Jezebel about the issue of idolatry, and compares Ahab to other kings of Israel.

My position is that rather than search for any number of reasons, which can easily turn into elaborate apologetics, it makes sense to accept the conclusion of critical research that a large part of this passage simply is not integral to the story but part of the editorial work.[9] It has been shown that the biblical literature underwent editorial processes over time; ignoring this possibility leads to a kind of scholarly one-sidedness that relies on rigid assumptions and seeks elaborate ways to justify the singularity of the received text, while ignoring the literary artistry of the biblical world, as well as the writers' intellectual world.[10] This is not to say that one must invariably adopt the conclusions of Bible criticism, but that it is best to take them into account.

Here is an example that ignores the conclusions of biblical research. Many scholars argue that the Song of Hannah (1 Sam 2:1-10) is not an integral part of the story of the birth of Samuel, mainly because its content is only loosely connected with Hannah's personal story and because it refers to a king in Israel ("He will give power to His king and triumph to His anointed one" [1 Sam 2:10]). Yet, the story is set in the time before the Israelite monarchy, and Hannah is not the barren woman who has borne seven (1 Sam 2:5).[11] Nevertheless, the reader need not regard this poem as out of place for several reasons: First, from the viewpoint of the plot, it is quite proper to include a prayer in the ceremony of dedicating a child to a shrine. Second, from the viewpoint of characterization, the prayer-song expresses the force of Hannah's personality and the way she sustains herself when parting from this child, for whose birth she had longed during her years of barrenness.[12] Third, from the viewpoint of poetics, such combinations of poetry, parable, riddle, ancient proverbs, and the like were quite popular with the biblical narrators.[13] Finally, from the reader's viewpoint, it appears that the Song of Hannah helps to present her behavior not as a tragic event but as an act of great faith.

Taking all these considerations into account and placing them against the common—probably mistaken—assumption that a story depicting a premonarchical period had to have been written in that period,[14] I maintain that it is possible to regard the poem as being an integral part of the story of the birth of Samuel, with the story and the poem forming one late work, which incorporates a version of a familiar hymn.[15]

The above examples, dealing variously with questions of text and editing, show how important it is not to launch into a thorough, professional study of the biblical story without first examining the text in the light of critical Bible research. A scholar who wishes to use the synchronic and diachronic methods of analysis in a complementary way can combine these two points of view.

Four

Beginnings and Endings

THUS FAR WE HAVE DISCUSSED THE OUTLINE of the story and the need to examine the demarcated unit in light of the findings of critical Bible research. We can now look at the way the stories open and close.

In most cases, the story opens with an exposition, which provides readers with the primary information and basic background materials to enable them to enter the world of the story, at least at the start.[1] These materials may present the central characters, refer to the time and/or place of the action, or depict the prevailing conditions and customs in the story's setting, which introduces the readers to a world that is differently constituted from their own. For example, the opening of the story of the Tower of Babel depicts a world that is unlike our own: "Everyone on earth had the same language and the same words . . ." (Gen 11:1).[2]

The exposition is usually made up of descriptive and static information, which can even be determined as habitual, and ends with the transition to the dynamic action in the form of some statement or deed that changes the initial situation. Consequently, the elements from which the exposition is constructed are different from those of the story itself. Continuing with the example of the Tower of Babel, we may define the exposition as going on to the end of verse 2 of Genesis 11: "And as they migrated from the east, they came upon a valley in the land of Shinar and settled there." This then was the opening setting: all the people speak the same language and live in the same valley of Shinar, and they will remain in that position until something happens or changes, which is the reason for writing the story. Had the situation remained unchanged, there would have been no story. But when the people began to say to each other, "Come, let us make bricks and burn them hard" (Gen 11:3), the story begins to move. The decision to manufacture bricks disrupts the calm depicted in the opening and leads in the end to a new reality. The people are no longer together in the valley, speaking a single language but scattered "over the face of the whole earth" (v. 8), and they no longer understand one another's speech (v. 9).

The elements making up the exposition are usually quite functional, serving the process of events. A typical example of this functionality is the opening of the story, which I have naturally entitled "Saul Visiting the Woman Necromancer" (1 Sam 28:3-25):

> Now Samuel had died and all Israel made lament for him; and he was buried in his own town of Ramah.[3] And Saul had forbidden [recourse to] ghosts and familiar spirits in the land. The Philistines mustered and they marched to Shunem and encamped; and Saul gathered all Israel and they encamped at Gilboa. When Saul saw the Philistine force, his heart trembled with fear. And Saul inquired of the LORD, but the LORD did not answer him, either by dreams or by Urim or by prophets. (vv. 3-6)[4]

This introduction contains all the important elements for the unfolding story. The report on the death of Samuel explains why it was necessary to conjure his spirit (v. 3a). The report on Saul's ban on necromancers (v. 3b) explains his subsequent behavior, when he needed to disguise himself to visit the woman necromancer. From the report on the two armies arranged face to face (v. 4), we learn that this is the eve of war and that Saul has evaluated the relative forces. We also learn about Saul's state of mind and the need for divine support. Finally, the reference to Saul's various efforts to inquire of the Lord (v. 6) reveals that this was not a single attempt but a series of failed attempts.

This state of affairs changes in verse 7, when the distraught Saul decides to act in a way that he himself condemned, since it was he who destroyed the necromancers. And yet here he is telling his servants to find a "woman who consults ghosts." It should be noted that the report about Samuel's death and burial had appeared before (1 Sam 25:1), in its apparently appropriate chronological position, before the story of David, Nabal the Carmelite, and Abigail. When readers reach the story about Saul and the woman necromancer, they should know that Samuel has died, but evidently the writer did not wish to rely upon the readers' memory and preferred to note Samuel's death by launching into the story of the conjuring of his ghost. If so, the repetition of this information has a functional reason.

Since the biblical narrative in the Pentateuch and the Former Prophets is a continuous sequence, beginning with the creation and ending with the fall of Jerusalem in the Book of Kings, an exposition is clearly called for in making the transition from one story to the next. Its purpose is to detach the readers from the materials they had been dealing with and introduce them to a new or different story world without losing their place in the sequence.[5] The story of Saul and the woman necromancer concludes with a concentric ending, which is typical of many biblical narratives. In this type of ending the hero turns back to the place he came from: Saul and his men who came to see the necromancer return to the camp at Gilboa where the Israelites are gathered.

The ending lowers the curtain, sends the players off the stage and behind the scenes, to another place and event, or, in the case of a concentric ending, back to where they came from: "Then they [Saul and his courtiers] rose and left the same night" (1 Sam 28:25b).[6] In the following story, dealing with David and Achish, the king of Gath (1 Samuel 29), the reader returns to the Philistines and to their preparations for the war against Israel under Saul's leadership, which naturally calls for a new exposition (1 Sam 29:1-2). This story reveals the differences of opinions in the Philistines' army. Although Achish wants David to take part in the war, his courtiers are totally against it. The story ends with the main parties remaining on stage but heading in different directions: "Accordingly, David and his men rose early in the morning to leave, to return to the land of the Philistines, while the Philistines marched up to Jezreel" (v. 11).

We may conclude that the exposition contains different kinds of details from those that appear in the body of the story, which describes the events. While the events are dynamic, the opening is descriptive, meaning that it is static, while the ending marks the exit of the personae and returns the reader to the static condition of the opening. Nevertheless, in a story with a concentric ending, the hero or heroes only seem to return to the condition from which they had set out, because the events have affected them—and the reader with them. The reality to which they return is not the same as it was. When Saul returned to the camp at Gilboa, he did not go back to the status quo but to a far harsher reality, because he had learned from the encounter with the spirit of Samuel at the necromancer's house exactly what fate lay in store for him, his sons, and the people of Israel. Now, the same reality appears much more frightening.

Similarly, Job—described at the opening of the book as "blameless and upright; he feared God and shunned evil," as well as a man of great wealth and the father of ten sons and daughters (Job 1:1-3)[7]—appears to return to a similar situation at the end of the book, but it is different. Job's wealth has doubled and he once again has ten sons and daughters; the daughters are the most beautiful in the land and inherit estates like their brothers (Job 42:12-16). This may seem to be the same Job whom we encountered at the beginning of the story. However, this is a Job who withstood the test, who can no longer be described merely as shunning evil, but as one who unwittingly confounded the heavenly adversary, the personification of evil, namely, Satan. We may reasonably assume that this Job is a different man. The ending of Job's story has one more characteristic feature of endings: the return to a static and calm situation, which is the new routine reality after the complication has been resolved.[8]

Since most biblical narratives are consecutive, the authors need provide only brief openings, as it is not necessary to reintroduce the characters anew with every story.[9]

Nevertheless, sometimes the opening words are extremely brief while also markedly directional. The story of the binding of Isaac opens with the words, "Some time afterward, God put Abraham to the test" (Gen 22:1a). The first part of this clause, "Some time afterward" (v. 1aa) is the editor's connecting statement, to indicate not only the new beginning but also the continuous quality of the narrative, showing that events happened in sequence. The exposition itself consists of the terse statement, "God put Abraham to the test" (v. 1ab).[10] The plot starts with God speaking to Abraham and presenting him with the frightful test: "Take your son, your favored one, Isaac, whom you love, and go to the land of Moriah, and offer him there as a burnt offering on one of the heights that I will point out to you" (v. 2). The exposition prepares the reader for a story with a motive of testing, a trial narrative. The reader knows who is about to test whom but not yet anything about the nature of the test, or if Abraham will pass it; but this opening has placed the matter of the test at the center of attention.

The story of the binding of Isaac, too, has a concentric ending —when Abraham has withstood the test and sacrificed the ram instead of his son, it is said: "Abraham then returned to his servants, and they departed together for Beersheba; and Abraham stayed in Beersheba" (v. 19). Abraham goes back to the place whence he came. The narrator repeats the word "together," but whereas before it was "the two [Abraham and Isaac] walked off together" (vv. 6, 8), now , in the ending, it is a general "departed together." This is not the terrified walk of the two leading personae—the father and the son, when the first knows the destination and the other does not know what to expect—but a general walk together, servants and all. It is a different walk, relieved of a burden; but who can tell what Abraham is feeling, despite having withstood the test, or Isaac, who just missed being sacrificed? They return to Beersheba. Isaac is not mentioned explicitly, but we can assume that he is there and that Abraham and Isaac are not the people they had been when they set out.[11]

In his book *The Story Begins,* Amos Oz states: "Any beginning of a story is always a kind of contract between writer and reader" (1999:7). He proceeds to itemize the types of "contracts": "Sometimes the opening paragraph or chapter works like a secret pact between writer and reader, behind the protagonist's back" (7). In this case the heroes are unaware that behind their backs writer and reader may exchange an amused wink at their expense. We find just such an agreement in another test undergone by Abraham, following which he was granted the birth of his son Isaac. The story in Gen 18:1-16 about the three angels who came to announce to Abraham the imminent birth of his son opens as follows: "The Lord appeared to him by the terebinths of Mamre; he was sitting at the entrance of the tent as the day grew hot" (v. 1). The attentive reader, conscious of the secret agreement, will realize that this is a story of a divine revelation. In this way, when the story proceeds to describe how Abraham looks up and sees three men standing near him, the reader realizes that the threesome are a trio representing the divine manifestation.[12] For Abraham, however, they are ordinary men, wearied by their journey and the heat of the day, who must be received hospitably and offered water to bathe their feet and food to restore their strength.

The reader, knowing that these are not mere wayfarers, can, like the divine threesome, observe the patriarch's hospitality while at the same time enjoying the idea of God's representatives bathing their feet and relishing a meal, which includes curds and milk with veal.

Amos Oz continues:

> There are beginnings that work rather like a honey trap: at first you are seduced with a juicy piece of gossip, or an all-revealing confession, or a bloodcurdling adventure, but eventually you find out that what you are getting is not a fish, but a stuffed fish . . . also many delicatessen items not mentioned on the menu, not even hinted at in the opening contract. (1999:8)

So it is in the opening of the story of Amnon and Tamar (2 Sam 13:1-22), which is a classic honey trap: "This happened sometime afterward: Absalom son of David had a beautiful sister named Tamar, and Amnon son of David became infatuated with her. Amnon was so distraught because of his [half-][13] sister Tamar that he became sick; for she was a virgin, and it seemed impossible to Amnon to do anything to her" (vv. 1-2).[14]

The first verse delivers fresh gossip from the royal court, a love story, pure honey—the prince Amnon loves the princess Tamar, who is Absalom's full sister. The second verse lays a trap that hints to the reader that this is not going to be a simple love story and that things are more complicated than they seem, without revealing that the "stuffing of the fish" is a tale of rape. This brief opening is a good example of the sophisticated use of language. Having declared the love in the first verse, the author musters several means—vocabulary, puns, associations, grammatical forms, and ambiguous syntax—to spring the trap of the love statement. The Hebrew text uses the root form *ṣrr* in describing Amnon's condition, which suggests that he was hard pressed yet also hints at lust.[15] Then the root form *ḥly* in the *hitpaʿel,* a reflexive conjugation, implies that his sickness might be feigned.[16] The circumstantial phrase, "for she was a virgin," may apply to what precedes it and to what follows. According to the first possibility, Amnon is sick because his sister is a virgin; and according to the second, it seems impossible for Amnon to do anything to her because she is a virgin.[17] The phrase "to do anything to her" (in Hebrew, *mᵉʾuma*) may mean either to do something or to do nothing. Does it mean that Tamar, being a virgin, is inaccessible, and Amnon cannot meet her and do anything to her? And what is that "anything"—a kiss on the cheek, a friendly chat, or something more?[18] In other words, the opening already makes it plain that this is not a disinterested love, otherwise why mention virginity, hint at lust, and end with "do anything to her"?

The end of the story (2 Sam 13:21-22) features the same four characters who figured in the exposition: David, Absalom, Amnon, and Tamar, but now their interrelationships are quite different.[19] David is angry and silent, while Absalom feels his sister's hurt and hates Amnon. There is no doubt that the reference to Absalom's hatred and its motivation with the words, "because he had violated his sister Tamar," are hints at future developments.

Oz states:

> Sometimes we are confronted with a harsh opening contract, almost forbidding, which warns the reader right from the outset: Tickets are very expensive here. If you feel you cannot afford a tough advance payment, you'd better not even try to get in. No concessions and no discounts are to be expected. (1999:8)

Such a "harsh opening contract" is the opening of the story of how Absalom's death was reported to his father David (2 Sam 18:19—19:1):[20] "Ahimaaz son of Zadok said, 'Let me run and report to the king that the Lord has vindicated him against his enemies'" (2 Sam 18:19). Young Ahimaaz does not realize that for David the joy of victory is the tragedy of losing his son. For Ahimaaz, Absalom is but one of the king's enemies, perhaps the worst of them. The reader, who remembers that David had warned Joab and Abishai and Ittai, "Deal gently with my boy Absalom, for my sake" (2 Sam 18:5; see also v. 12), knows that what will follow will be a harsh story about the announcement of a dreadful blow.

Then "there are philosophical contracts," continues Oz, quoting the famous opening sentence of *Anna Karenina* by Leo Tolstoy.[21] One such "philosophical" opening, dealing with human existence, is the long introduction (Gen 2:4b—3:1a)[22] to the story of the Garden of Eden (Gen 2:4b—3:24).[23] The story opens with the circumstances of the creation of the garden and ends with the expulsion of the humans from it. The humans are forced to leave the paradisiacal environment and to live in the outside world, which is described at the beginning of the story thus: "when no shrub of the field was yet on earth and no grasses of the field had yet sprouted, because the LORD God had not sent rain upon the earth and there was no man to till the soil" (Gen 2:5). This story also has a concentric ending; the curse laid on man returns him to the place to which God had not wished to bring him:

> Cursed be the ground because of you. . . .
> Thorns and thistles shall it sprout for you.
> But your food shall be the grasses of the field; . . .
> Until you return to the ground—
> For from it you were taken.
> For dust you are,
> And to dust you shall return. (Gen 3:17-19)[24]

These opening verses alone tell us how the author views life in the world outside the Garden of Eden and the place of humans in it, but the theme is developed further later in the exposition.

The reader can see at a glance that this is an unusually lengthy exposition. The plot begins at the start of chapter 3: the serpent entices the woman (3:1b-2), she eats of the forbidden fruit, she gives it to her husband, their eyes are opened, and they are punished and expelled from the garden forever. While the story itself encompasses chapter 3, the opening covers almost a whole chapter—from the second half of verse 4 in chapter 2 to the first half of verse 1 in chapter 3—which is an exposition of twenty verses for a plot of twenty-four verses.

A closer look reveals that this lengthy exposition contains elements that are not relevant to the story. Everything to do with the Garden of Eden, its personae and the laws governing life in it, are expositionary elements. But whatever does not serve the tale of sin and punishment, or meets the functional principle, cannot be regarded as expositionary, and we must wonder what it is doing here.

The expositionary elements are the descriptions of the world before the creation of man (2:4b-6), the creation of man and of the garden and its flora and the two special trees within it—the tree of life and the tree of the knowledge of good and evil (vv. 7-9); the laws governing life in the garden, according to which man is employed "to till it and tend it" (v. 15). In addition, man must observe the divine commandment: "Of every tree of the garden you are free to eat, but as for the tree of the knowledge of good and bad, you must not eat of it; for as soon as you eat of it, you shall die" (vv. 16-17); the creation of animals—including the serpent—and of the woman (vv. 18, 19 [until the words "all the wild beasts"], 20b, 21-23), as those who were intended to be "a fitting helper for him"; and finally the representation of the acting personae: man, woman, and the serpent (2:25; 3:1a). Close attention to the laws governing life in the Garden of Eden leads to the conclusion that although life in the Garden of Eden is represented as the ideal existence, the author evidently does not regard idleness and slackness as ideals. That is why man works even in paradise, "to till it and tend it," and here too he must obey the divine commandments. Anarchy is not an ideal, and the Garden of Eden is not anarchic. Moreover, life in it is eternal. Only the violation of the divine ordinance and the eating of the forbidden fruit canceled the promise of immortality that the Garden of Eden held for man. That is why the story concludes with the statement: "He drove the man out, and stationed east of the garden of Eden the cherubim and the fiery ever-turning sword, to guard the way to the tree of life" (3:24). Finally, the description of the relationship between man and woman lacks sexual tension: both were naked, "yet they felt no shame" (2:25).

On the other hand, the introduction also contains information that could be dispensed with, because it is not necessary to the rest of the story. Such is the description of the rivers outside the garden and their courses (2:10-14); the description of man naming the animals (vv. 19 [from the words "all the birds of the sky"] to 20a), and finally, the anachronistic verse that describes the life outside the garden and after the curses: "Hence a man leaves his father and mother and clings to his wife, so that they become one flesh" (v. 24). But even without these eight verses, it is still a lengthy introduction. We must therefore seek an answer to the following two questions: Why is this introduction so long? Why does it include elements that have nothing to do, as an exposition, with the rest of the story?

This exposition depicts a kind of utopia, an ideal world that man has lost by his misconduct. By depicting such a utopian world the author implies his criticism of the existing world in which human beings have been condemned to live ever since the expulsion.[25] The keen reader will soon perceive that the Garden of Eden never existed but is a parable of a utopia.[26] This conclusion is supported by any attempt to figure out the geography of the story, which is doomed to failure. According to the story, the garden is located at the junction of the Pishon, whose location no one knows, which "winds through the whole land of Havilah" (Saudi Arabia?), the Gihon (either the stream near Jerusalem or some other), that "winds through the whole land of Cush" (in Africa?), and the Tigris and the Euphrates (see p. 121 below). In other words, there is no point in looking for the garden, for it is a utopia, a not-place (*ou-tópos* in Greek). But like all utopias, its purpose is to criticize the existing world and depict a place where conditions are ideal. The exposition of the story of the Garden of Eden is designed to show us what is bad in our world and what is good, or what is needed for a harmonious existence. Whatever is outside the garden is bad—including the gold of the land of Havilah and its gems. Man and wife roamed about the garden naked and unashamed, their eyes had not yet opened to the differences between the genders, which means that sexual awareness does not belong to the routine of the garden. Above all, the garden is free of the curses that represent humanity's struggle for survival, in which man struggles against the animal world, rules over woman, and eats by the sweat of his brow until he dies. The garden is thus a kind of ideal childhood, though not an unruly one, for it entails work for preservation and pleasure, obedience to God, the avoidance of materialist values (such as gold, bdellium, and lapis lazuli), life with a helpmeet, without fear of death and without sexual tension, but with man having an advantage over his environment since he is the name-giver.[27]

Here the introduction is long because the author uses it not only to introduce functional information but to summarize a philosophical discourse in which he poses the negative elements (money, represented by gold and by precious stones; sex, represented by being naked; work for survival, represented by work for preservation and pleasure; and finally death, represented by the tree of life) against the world of the lost childhood, which is governed by a different order, characterized by the absence of materialist values: "games" of tilling and tending, innocence, and immortality.

We see that in the Bible, too, the opening of a story is almost always a contractual agreement between the writer and the reader, not a single, fixed contract form, but a variety of them—and every contract has an ending as well.

Five

Plots, Structures, and Their Functions

ACCORDING TO ARISTOTLE, every story "has beginning, middle and end" (*Poetics* 7.26–27). We have discussed the endings and, especially, the beginnings; now we shall look at the middle, namely, the body of the story.

> A story relates what is happening to people, and describes objects, places and events. However, not every description is necessarily a story. What makes a description into a story is a significant change: a bad situation is improved (for instance, when one of the characters overcomes a rival or a difficult obstacle); a situation which was good at the outset grows markedly worse (for instance, due to a failure, or being hurt by a rival). In a story, the main thing is the change, the event which makes the reader feel that something has occurred. (Polak 1994:1)

The change is communicated through the plot, which is a series of events, an account of what happened. The plot is a selection and organization of events in a particular order of time; it is a purposeful structure built around the conflict between the personae, or it may be the internal conflict of one character. The author, who has a purpose in mind, selects a series of events out of countless possibilities and decides how to organize them, what comes after what. The author can organize them in chronological order or may deviate from it and anticipate later events, or introduce at some late stage in the sequence developments that were, chronologically speaking, earlier. When the author chooses to present the story in a causal sequence, the events will naturally appear in chronological order. The biblical stories, which are set in a historiographic framework, are generally faithful to the chronological organization, as befits a historical description.

To make a story accessible to the readership, the author usually constructs the plot in three stages: the first is the stage of complication, which reveals how and why the opening conditions have changed. Having set out the background elements in the exposition, the author introduces the complication, or crisis, which brings on the change. Following the change, which is the second stage and the heart of the story, comes the third stage, the unraveling, in which the consequences of the change are revealed. When we add the exposition and the ending to these three stages, we get a five-stage structure, arranged symmetrically and governed by a concentric structure, though some describe it as a pediment.[1]

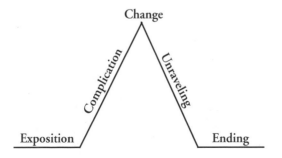

The Pediment Structure

Applying the structure of the pediment, with its emphasis on the change, makes it possible to analyze any story, in the Bible or elsewhere. Let us examine two biblical stories with regard to this sequence of stages: the Tower of Babel and the Victory of Ehud son of Gera.

In the story of the Tower of Babel (Gen 11:1-9), during the expository stage, which we have previously touched on (p. 33), all the people speak one language and live in a valley in the land of Shinar. The stage of complication that leads to the change is the plan to make bricks and use them to build a tower with its top in the sky, "else we shall be scattered all over the world" (v. 4b). The change takes place when God comes down to look at the handiwork and decides to prevent the people from carrying out their project. The resolution occurs when God confounds their speech and scatters them over the face of the earth. The story concludes with a name etymology and a note on the new state of affairs: "That is why it was called Babel, because there the LORD confounded the speech of the whole earth, and from there the LORD scattered them over the face of the whole earth" (v. 9).

Another example is the story of Ehud son of Gera (Judg 3:12-30). The exposition depicts a state of submission that lasted eighteen years. It also presents the personae: the sinful Israelites, God who punishes them and surrenders them to Eglon (king of Moab), Eglon and his military achievements, and finally, the figure chosen by God to be the Israelites' champion, Ehud son of Gera, a left-handed man. The customary state of affairs is that the subject people pay the conquering king a tax in the form of a tribute that they present to him, and here it is Ehud who leads the delegation of the tribute bearers. The complication begins when Ehud decides to make a special kind of dagger and slips it into the palace when he and his men bring the tribute. The turning point occurs when Ehud remains alone with the king in the cool upper chamber, kills him with the hidden dagger, and flees from the palace. The resolution takes place when Ehud succeeds in getting back to the Israelite side in time, mustering an army, and freeing Israel from the Moabite domination (this is made possible because, while Ehud was fleeing, the king's servants tarried, failing to realize that he had been killed). The conclusion depicts a new routine situation, when the land is at peace for eighty years.

The Scenic Character

A close look at the plots of the biblical stories reveals that, as well as the classical pediment structure we have just observed, there are other methods of analysis that can contribute to the understanding of narrative plots and their implication—for example, the method that studies the scenic structuring of biblical narrative. This is a way of examining the unfolding of the plot, first in terms of the transitions of time, place, and character, and also in terms of distinguishing between "telling" and "showing." The "telling" has the character of a report. The narrator describes what is happening and does not let the personae speak for themselves. The reader gets the information indirectly, through a "middleman," the narrator, and without the intervention of the personae. A unit shaped as a report can be characterized by the narrator's intervening, explicating, summarizing, or evaluating. By contrast, a unit of "showing" is more like a dramatic scene—it is the most direct presentation possible, with hardly any intervention by the narrator. In such a unit the events are presented by the personae themselves, and the narrator's mediation is reduced to a minimum. A story unit characterized as "showing" is more dramatic and creates a more credible impression, as if that is precisely how things happened or precisely what the characters said.[2] Stories are rarely exclusively "showing" (that is most often found in drama). While a play is generally made up entirely of "showing," in stories the two modes intertwine.[3] When the narrator allows the personae to communicate, he seems to be giving them the floor, though without disappearing altogether, but remaining on the spot to report who is speaking: so-and-so said, so-and-so responded. This enables the readers to hear the characters almost without the narrator's intervention. Biblical stories are always a combination of reports, which are characterized by "telling," and discourses, the latter being mainly "showing." The determination where one unit ends and another begins within the story, whether of "telling" or of "showing," is a matter of alteration—alteration in time, place, and/or personae.

The story of Othniel son of Kenaz (Judg 3:7-11) is an example of a short story that is all report; thus, the change it depicts lacks all dramatic tone. We are told that the Israelites did what was offensive to the Lord, who surrendered them to Cushan-rishataim, king of Aram-naharaim, who subjugated them for eight years. They cried out to the Lord, who raised a champion to deliver them, Othniel son of Kenaz. The spirit of the Lord descended upon him, he went out to war, overcame Cushan-rishataim, and the land had peace for forty years. All this is told by the narrator; the voices of the persons involved are never heard.

The extreme shortness of this story is not what caused it to be written entirely as "telling" or report. The story of Samson and the gates of Gaza (Judg 16:1-3), which is discussed in chapter 1, is a mere three verses long, yet the narrator enables us twice to hear the characters speak, both times on the Philistine side. The first time we hear the news that reached the Gazites: "The Gazites [learned] that Samson had come there" (v. 2).[4] Then we hear the Philistines whispering and plotting to kill Samson in the morning: "they gathered and lay in ambush for him in the town gate the whole night; and all night long they kept whispering to each other, 'When daylight comes, we'll kill him'" (v. 2). Letting the Philistines speak for themselves about their plan to capture Samson, while Samson has been gone since midnight, makes them appear ridiculous. On the other hand, the narrator's dry tone when he reports Samson's deed emphasizes the ease with which he pulled out the city gates and made off with them to the top of the mountain near Hebron. Thus the choice between "telling" and "showing" is not a question of the length of the story but of the author's intention. The more the author wishes to make the story dramatic, the more he reduces the narration and allows the personae to speak for themselves.[5]

The story of Abraham's purchase of the Cave of Machpelah (Genesis 23) is almost entirely "showing." Aside from the exposition and the conclusion, which are in report form as usual, the body of the story is one long scene describing the negotiations between purchaser and sellers, and the narrator gives the floor to speaker after speaker. In this story there are no changes of place or characters: the negotiations between Abraham and the Hittites take place in a single session, in the same place, and among the same group of people. Depicting the interaction in a single scene intensifies the dramatic impact of the discourse, with the fine nuances that each side gives it. A break in the negotiations would weaken their impact as a psychodynamic process in which both sides are unwilling to retreat. Interrupting the process could cause the sides to become entrenched in their initial positions, so it is imperative to keep the process going until an outcome is agreed upon. This is what happens in life, and we recognize it in the lifelike world depicted in the story because the author made sure to compress it into a single continuous scene. A closer look at the positions of the various speakers reveals the process and the author's preference for a single long scene.[6]

Genesis 23:1-2 is the exposition that provides the background information. Sarah has died and Abraham wishes to bury her. The concentric ending of the story, verses 19-20, reports the burial of Sarah and Abraham's acquisition of the field with its cave as a burial site. In between stretches a single scene that opens with

Abraham approaching the Hittites and presenting his request. Abraham opens by stating that he is a "resident alien," meaning that he is aware of his status as a stranger who resides in the place but has no right to land,[7] and is therefore dependent on the goodwill of the local landowners, the Hittites.[8] Having thus prevented them from putting him in his place and reminding him of his status, he puts his request in a simple, general form: "Sell me a burial site among you, that I may remove my dead for burial" (v. 4b).[9] The mention of a burial site makes it explicit that he means a plot of land, not merely a grave. The root *ntn* can be interpreted either as giving a gift or "giving" to a buyer "at the full price," namely selling.[10] At this stage Abraham is being vague so that his interlocutors would be unable to say: No, we cannot sell to you, since you have no right to buy. The Hittites respond to Abraham with courtesy and respect: "Hear us, my lord, you are the elect of God among us" (v. 6a).[11] Offering him a choice of any grave he wants, they add, "None of us will withhold his burial place from you for burying your dead" (v. 6b).

These courtesies, containing nothing specific, enable Abraham to appeal to the people of the land, the Hittites, who are the leaders of the town. He too bows courteously but proceeds to be specific: "If it is your wish that I remove my dead for burial, you must agree to intercede for me with Ephron son of Zohar" (v. 7). In other words, if you are sincere in wishing to help me, let me speak to Ephron son of Zohar. Abraham probably had Ephron's site in mind, because it was located "at the edge of his land," possibly on the town boundary, as implied by verse 17, which notes that the Cave of Machpelah was "near Mamre."[12] Such a location would make the field easily accessible.[13] Moreover, Abraham emphasizes that he wishes to pay the full price for the burial site, meaning the plot of land that contained the Cave of Machpelah. Ephron, who is present, responds unctuously that he is willing to give Abraham the field and the cave, in the presence of witnesses, for the purpose of burial. Ephron, too, uses the verb root *ntn* (to give), without referring explicitly to a purchase. Now Abraham bows low to the people of the land and says to Ephron: "Let me pay the price of the land; accept it from me, that I may bury my dead there" (v. 13b). He is making clear that by "giving" he means purchase for money, both sides knowing that buying the land means also buying the cave. Thus Abraham enables Ephron to name any price that occurs to him, which is obviously too great a temptation to resist. Ephron quotes what was probably a very large sum, saying, "A piece of land worth four hundred shekels of silver, what is it between you and me? Go and bury your dead" (v. 15), implying that the quoted value is not too high for the right to buy local land.[14] Abraham seizes the moment, as he is determined to buy the land, and instead of continuing the dialogue, at once pays out the amount everyone had heard quoted. The purchase takes place in the presence of the townspeople at the town gate, which is also the place of judgment. The legal transaction itemizes everything that is included in the purchase: "the field with its cave and all the trees anywhere within the confines of that field" (v. 17).

Breaking up such a story into a series of scenes would have destroyed the dynamic of the negotiation. The author wished to show how Abraham, though having no rights, succeeded in legally purchasing a piece of land from the landowners of Hebron. Clearly this purchase was regarded as extremely important by the editors of the Book of Genesis, as it is mentioned on three further occasions: in connection with the burial of Abraham (25:9-10), with Jacob's will (49:29-32), and with Jacob's burial (50:13), each time referring explicitly to the details of the purchase and property rights.[15] Since the issue was important, the author saw fit to clarify how Abraham succeeded in purchasing a piece of land in Hebron legally, in the presence of witnesses. To do this to the best effect, he chose to present it in a single continuous scene that conveys the atmosphere of the negotiations.

An example of a story in which the transition from one scene to the next is significant is that of Naboth the Jezreelite (1 Kings 21).[16]

This story also deals with the acquisition of a piece of land but now in an illegitimate way, entailing transitions and changes of location, time, and the dramatic personae. Here the examination of the scene structure is useful to the understanding of the whole story.

The story begins with an expository unit in the form of a report by the narrator. Overlooking the opening editorial phrase, "The following events occurred sometime afterward,"[17] the reader proceeds to the exposition itself: "Naboth the Jezreelite owned a vineyard in Jezreel, adjoining the palace of King Ahab of Samaria" (v. 1).[18] This brief exposition, a unit reported by the narrator, communicates much more than meets the eye. The statement that Naboth's vineyard in Jezreel adjoined the palace of the king of Samaria suggests not only that Ahab had two palaces, one in Samaria and one in Jezreel,[19] but that the latter was worthy of the title *hekal*, a term generally used for a temple of God in biblical literature.[20] Thus, while the statement points to the relative value of a vineyard versus palace, and a citizen versus king, it also contains a veiled criticism of the king who made his house into a temple.[21] As an exposition, this unit is static in nature.

The first scene (vv. 2-3) takes place in the vineyard itself. King Ahab makes his material offer to buy the vineyard and turn it into a vegetable garden, and Naboth responds by expressing his profound attachment to his ancestral land. The king realizes that it is useless to try to persuade Naboth or start negotiating and goes home furious.

The next scene (vv. 4-10) opens in a different location with new characters. It is set in the king's place, or to be precise, the private room that contains his bed, with Ahab and his wife Jezebel present. In this scene of dialogue Ahab convinces Jezebel that a terrible wrong has been done to him. He does not report exactly what took place in the vineyard but describes the event in terms that are sure to incense Jezebel. He tells her that he offered Naboth everything possible, money or another vineyard, and that Naboth responded rudely and arbitrarily: "I will not give my vineyard to you" (v. 6b). Queen Jezebel is horrified by the conduct of the subject Naboth to the king of Israel and declares to her husband: "Now is the time to show yourself king over Israel" (v. 7a); she promises to obtain the vineyard for him. She takes the king's seal and writes letters to the elders and nobles who live in Naboth's town.[22] The narrator quotes her instructions: "Proclaim a fast and seat Naboth at the front of the assembly. And seat two scoundrels opposite him, and let them testify against him: 'You have reviled God and king!' Then take him out and stone him to death" (vv. 9-10). The letters give detailed instructions for a careful staging of a show trial for Naboth. Jezebel makes sure to make this a public issue, based on the claim that the accused man cursed the king, who is God's elect.[23] She demands that two men bear false witnesses against Naboth, since "a case can be valid only on the testimony of two witnesses or more" (Deut 19:15b),[24] determines what the punishment must be, how it is to be executed, and even demands that the execution by stoning be confirmed to her.

The third scene (vv. 11-14), which lies at the heart of this story, describes how Jezebel's instructions were carried out to the letter. The narrator is so keen to make this clear to the reader that he repeats himself, noting that the elders "did as Jezebel had instructed them, just as was written in the letters she had sent them: They proclaimed a fast . . ." (vv. 11-12), and so on.[25] This time he does not give the floor to the personae, but he himself reports how everything she had written was carried out exactly. Nevertheless, for the sake of dramatic authenticity, he interpolates a quote that, naturally, is the false accusation leveled against Naboth, as testified by the scoundrels: "Naboth has reviled God and king" (v. 13). This scene takes place in Naboth's town, Jezreel, and ends with the confirmation sent to Jezebel: "Naboth has been stoned to death" (v. 14).

The fourth scene (vv. 15-16), which corresponds to the second (vv. 4-10), takes place in the king's palace. Jezebel says to Ahab, "Go and take possession of the vineyard which Naboth the Jezreelite refused to sell you for money; for Naboth is no longer alive, he is dead" (v. 15). Ahab rises, snaps out of his bedridden depression, and like a little boy goes off to play with the new "toy" that "mama" Jezebel has gotten for him.

The fifth scene (vv. 17-27), corresponding to the first (vv. 2-3), takes place in the vineyard once again: Ahab and Elijah meet there. Elijah, whom God instructed to reprove the king with the phrase, "Would you murder and take possession?" (v. 19), carries out the divine command precisely and even informs the king that he would die in the land of Naboth the Jezreelite.[26] The scene ends with the narrator's report about Ahab's reaction. Having heard Elijah's harsh prophecy, the king tears his clothes, puts on sackcloth (a sign of mourning), and observes other mourning customs, such as fasting.

The end of this story is also in scene form ("showing"): the Lord says to Elijah that because Ahab humbled himself before God, the disaster would not come in his lifetime but that of his son.[27] In this way the author adjusts the story to fit with what he knows from the Book of Kings; specifically, that it was actually Ahab's son Joram who was killed by Jehu in the field of Naboth the Jezreelite (2 Kings 9:24-26).

We have seen that the story is made up of five scenes, arranged in a concentric order. The symmetry becomes more visible when we describe the scenes by their settings: vineyard, palace, place of judgment, palace, vineyard. This is called a concentric structure: A, B, x, B, A, with x as the core.[28] If we observe all the units of the story, including the exposition and conclusion, we get the following structure: A, B, C, x, C, B, A.

I would add that the division into structural units of scenes can correspond with the classic pediment structure, as in this story. According to the pediment structure, the story is also divided into five units, organized symmetrically: an introduction that sets out the starting conditions; followed by the complication—the king wants the vineyard and involves his wife; change—the killing of Naboth in a show trial for the purpose of seizing his land;

resolution—the king will not inherit the vineyard and will be punished for permitting the murder; conclusion—the king's remorse and the transferal of the punishment to his son.[29]

Both methods of analyzing the plot are legitimate, while each of them reveals a particular aspect. The classical pediment structure emphasizes the background to the conflict, its climax, and its unraveling, whereas the observation of scenes and the transitions from "telling" to "showing" draws out other aspects, such as the various personae, their distinct roles, their respective involvement, and their contribution to the progress of the plot, the locations, the discourses, their effectiveness, and the like. The reader can choose which method to apply—that is, on which to focus the observation, and as always two—or more—are better than one.

⌒

Examining the units of the Naboth story from the viewpoint of the placement of the characters and their deployment reveals that the symmetrical organization has a meaning and a clear purpose. In the exposition, Ahab, the king and owner of the palace, is represented vis-à-vis Naboth, the citizen and owner of the vineyard. In the first scene, when Ahab asks Naboth to sell him the vineyard, they are the active characters. In the second scene, when Ahab turns the problem over into Jezebel's harsh hands, he and Jezebel are the moving characters. In the third and central scene, that of the show trial, the active characters are Naboth, the scoundrels, the townspeople, and the elders, who presumably acted as judges, while in the background lurks the image of Ahab, the source of the accusation. The fourth scene, which parallels the second, again features Ahab and Jezebel, the latter announcing the successful execution of her scheme. In the fifth scene, which parallels the first, Ahab is again in the vineyard; only in place of the dead Naboth, Elijah appears as God's emissary, sent to avenge the murdered man in the same place. Ahab, who regrets his deed, is the subject of God's speech to Elijah in the ending of the story.

This arrangement would seem deliberate and not accidental or random—it tells us how the author viewed the role of Ahab, who is mentioned in every unit, including the exposition and the ending. Ahab wanted the vineyard, and he did not prevent Jezebel from using his seal. The trial took place because Jezebel sent letters signed with the king's seal—signifying that it took place under the king's aegis—then Jezebel, acting as the king's agent, informed him that his wish had been fulfilled. Finally, the charge "Would you murder and take possession?" was thrown at Ahab, not at Jezebel, and in the end Ahab is described as the one who feels remorse and therefore deserves God's mercy. The exposition, the scene of the trial, which is the heart of the story, and the ending—important units from the structural point of view—are concerned with Ahab and do not even mention Jezebel. The story's scenic structure, which determines who the active characters are and where and how they appear, is therefore highly functional. It indicates that Jezebel, for all her efficiency, could not have done what she did except in the name of the king and with his authority. Some readers have even concluded that she was being manipulated by Ahab.[30] Thus, the placement of the characters and their deployment has a clear function: to emphasize that the responsibility for the murder of Naboth falls wholly on King Ahab.

Units and Transitions

An interesting example of the functional use of the unit structure, notably the transition from one unit to the next, is the story of the victory of Ehud son of Gera (Judg 3:12-30). Here an examination of the changes of time, place, and/or the protagonists within the outlined story reveals five units, each representing one of the tactics used by Ehud, whether plotted in advance, improvised on the spot in unforeseen circumstances, or because the circumstances had been manipulated for him.[31]

The first unit (v. 16) contains an exact description of the special dagger that Ehud planned and prepared for himself: a very small dagger (in Hebrew, *gomɛd*),[32] having two edges and therefore a great penetrating capacity. Ehud hides the dagger under his cloak and, being left-handed, tucks it on his right side. This reported unit presumably takes place in some secret place and devoid of witnesses. Ehud clearly has a secret plan involving his hidden dagger.

In the second unit (vv. 17-18), which takes place in the hall of tribute, in the presence of many people, the reader is subtly informed, by means of sophisticated wording, about Ehud's tactics during the presentation of the tribute: "When [Ehud] had finished presenting the tribute, he dismissed the people who had conveyed the tribute" (v. 18). This wording suggests that the payment of tribute was a ceremony with a beginning, a middle, and an end, and only when it ended did Ehud dismiss the people—in Hebrew the word *ʿam* suggests that it was a numerous company that had come to present the tribute to the conquering monarch. A sense of the ceremonial also arises from the phrase used in the Hebrew for "bring the tribute" (*lᵉhakriv ʾet hamminḥa*), with its connotations of religious ritual (it can also mean "to offer a cereal sacrifice"). These are intensified by the repetition of the name Eglon, resembling *ʿegel*, meaning a calf, which hints that in this case the king will be the sacrificial calf (Alter 1981:39). Ceremonies usually last a long time, and time was important to Ehud, which is why he brought a good deal of tribute whose presentation would be lengthy. This way he creates the impression that he is a loyal subject, humble and devoted to the conquering king. By dismissing his companions and presumably remaining on his own, he must have reinforced the impression that he is a harmless and nonthreatening presence, and this calculated conduct probably enabled him to reach the cool upper chamber, occupied by the king alone.

The third unit, which is also the central one and marks the change (vv. 19-23), describes how Ehud remains alone with the king in the cool chamber, gets him to rise from his seat, and kills him. This scene is replete with tactics. Ehud tells the king that he has a secret message for him, causing the king to send his attendants out of the room and leaving the two of them alone. The next tactic is to get the king to rise. The king was very fat, and if he remained seated, the dagger might not have reached his internal organs, but if he stood up, the dagger would pierce through. So Ehud tells the king that he has brought a message from God, in honor of which the king rises. Having stabbed the king, Ehud improvises the tactic of hiding the murder weapon by leaving it buried in the folds of the king's belly. Finally, he leaves through the main door, which can be locked after him, rather than through a window, without arousing suspicion.[33]

The fourth unit (vv. 24-26) depicts the attendants arriving as Ehud left. They assume that the meeting is over and that the king is still occupied with some personal issues (evacuating himself), so they avoid disturbing him. Simultaneously Ehud takes advantage of the interval to get away. Thus, in this scene the action takes place in two parallel settings: one is outside the locked door in the palace, and the other is the route of Ehud's flight.

The fifth unit (vv. 27-29) deals with the final tactic, that of the war itself. Ehud urges his men to capture the fords of the Jordan and prevent the Moabites from fleeing. As a result, ten thousand Moabites were killed that day.

Here, too, we can distinguish a symmetrical vertex that reveals the different tactics. The apex is the third scene, that of the murder, which made up of a series of tactics. Also, the first and fifth tactic are directly connected with killing the enemy (the dagger and the war); while the second tactic (the presentation of the tribute) and the fourth (the attendants waiting outside the locked door) prepare the ground for what follows: murder and war.

But something else happens in this story. The transition from unit to unit indicates the progress of the plot, which the reader is unable to visualize in the absence of informative data and the details required to bridge the gaps in order to reconstruct the event. There is no information between the preparation of the dagger and the scene of the tribute to tell us how Ehud came to be in the palace. Between the tribute and the murder scenes there is nothing to tell us how Ehud managed to get into the cool upper chamber, which was reserved for the exclusive use of the king. After the murder it remains unclear how the door that was shut after Ehud's departure was also locked, so that the servants who arrived the moment Ehud left, not a minute earlier, found a locked door. Again, it is not clear how the fleeing Ehud had enough time to reach Mount Ephraim, rally the army, and seize the fords of the Jordan before the Moabites reached them. When we examine these transitions we find that there are many gaps in the story, particularly in the passage from unit to unit. This gives the reader a feeling of being dropped from one unit into the heart of another, having skipped over the intervening stages. A series of such cumulative drops creates a significant effect—it suggests that someone has taken care of the intervening stages, put the events in motion, and orchestrated their timing. In this way, the many-gapped scene structure of this story underlines the central role the author has assigned to God: God creates the circumstances, and God makes the tactics succeed. Ehud may devise them, but their effectiveness depends on God's will and power. In fact, the author informs us about God's place in the story right at the start, when he says, "The LORD let King Eglon of Moab prevail over Israel" (v. 12). In other words, Eglon's military achievements and the defeat of Israel are not the consequences of the Moabite king's strength and abilities, but of the will of the God of Israel. Ehud acknowledges this in the fifth scene, when he addresses his army with the words, "The LORD has delivered your enemies, the Moabites, into your hands" (v. 28). Having learned to what extent God has helped him, he now passes this conclusion to his men. This essential message is also passed to the reader by means of the structure, which emphasizes the gaps, the tactics, and the significance of their systematic success.

The Three-and-Four Structure

The scene-based structure is not the only functional type. Let us now examine another structure, the three-and-four structure, which occurs many times in the various genres of biblical literature.[34] As we shall see, this structure is often used to convey confrontation and persuasion and for effecting a change of attitude. It entails four events sharing a common denominator, the last of which entails a change in position; in other words, after three ineffective occurrences, there is an effective fourth.

The first example is Jotham's parable (Judg 9:7-21), which represents this three-and-four pattern briefly and clearly. The parable describes four attempts at persuasion: three failed and the fourth was successful. The parable opens with the words, "Once the trees went to anoint a king over themselves" (v. 8)—stating the common wish for a king and the need to persuade one of them to take on the task. The olive tree declined, for reasons of its own, the fig tree likewise, and so did the vine. But the fourth, the thornbush, behaved differently—after stating its conditions and issuing a warning, it accepted the proposal. The thornbush's agreement to reign over the trees is notable by contrast with the refusal of the three productive trees and hints at a pejorative view of monarchy and kings.[35]

The same structure occurs in the story of Samson and Delilah (Judg 16:4-21), where Delilah tries to get Samson to tell her the secret of his extraordinary strength.[36] Verse 4, which is the exposition, opens with the editor's connecting phrase "After that" and then describes a new situation in Samson's life: "he fell in love with a woman in the Wadi Sorek, named Delilah." The novelty is that, unlike Samson's previous relations with women, here he is in love. The narrator does not need to name Samson, because the reader of this cycle of stories, which began in chapter 13, knows who the subject is. However, he does introduce Delilah, a new feminine personage in the tale of Samson's exploits. The plot begins with a description of the lords of the Philistines coming to Delilah and proposing that she coax Samson and discover the secret of his strength, so that they may overpower him. They naturally offer her a vast amount of money for her help: "we'll each give you eleven hundred shekels of silver" (v. 5b)—presumably a total of five thousand five hundred silver shekels.[37]

From here on the story sticks to the three-and-four structure. Delilah tries Samson three times, three times she fails (vv. 6-9, 10-12, 13-14), the fourth time she succeeds (vv. 15-21a). The reader perceives this structure not only because of the plot development that I have outlined but also because of the phrasing. While each unit describes an attempt carried out in a different way, the wording is similar, so the reader cannot be unaware of the distinctive structure. In the first attempt Delilah begins by saying, "Tell me, what makes you so strong? And how could you be tied up and made helpless?" (v. 6). The second time: "Oh, you deceived me; you lied to me! Do tell me now how you could be tied up" (v. 10). The third time, "You have been deceiving me all along; you have been lying to me! Tell me, how you could be tied up" (v. 13). But note the fourth: "How can you say you love me, when you don't confide in me? This makes three times that you've deceived me and haven't told me what makes you so strong" (v. 15). This time, the narrator, wishing to explain why Samson revealed his secret, adds his own comment: "Finally, after she had nagged him and pressed him constantly, he was wearied to death and he confided everything to her" (vv. 15-16). In such a story there must be a convincing element of persuasion; the reader must understand why Samson was persuaded to break his vow and risk his life. To achieve this, the narrator uses the three-and-four structure, which is often used for persuasion, as well as his own commentary. It is worth noting that this structure also strengthens the effect of tension. The reader waits impatiently for the change.

There is no point in analyzing this story in terms of its scene structure because of the multiplicity of scenes that fall into the proposed three-and-four division and also because the transition from one scene-unit to the other is not distinct. An application of the pediment structure to this story would reveal that its center of gravity—or the change—is not in the middle but near the end of the story, in the fourth stage, and that the story lacks the stage of unraveling. Applying the three-and-four pattern to this story brings out the dynamic that leads up to Samson revealing his secret, as well as the subtle changes in phrasing at each of the four stages.

The same pattern is used ironically in the story of Job, in the description of the catastrophes that befall him (Job 1:13-22).[38] The first messenger reports a loss of property. While he is speaking, another messenger arrives and reports further loss of property. While this one is speaking, a third arrives and reports still more damage to property, and finally the fourth one arrives and reports that Job's sons and daughters are dead. At this point Job tears his robe, cuts off his hair, and bows down, saying, "Naked came I out of my mother's womb, and naked shall I return there; the LORD has given and the LORD has taken away; blessed be the name of the LORD" (1:21). In addition to the cumulative effect of three and even four disasters, it is ironic that all these disasters could not bring Job to sin: "For all that, Job did not sin nor did he cast reproach on God" (v. 22). Moreover, they did not persuade God that there was no need to put Job to the test, but only persuaded Satan to try additional ways of tormenting him. The ironic use of the pattern in this case persuades the reader that he may criticize God's acquiescence.

The story of Amnon and Tamar is also an interesting example of the three-and-four pattern of organizing the units composing it.[39] The story is made up of four scenes: the first is the meeting of Amnon and Jonadab (vv. 3-5); the second is the meeting between Amnon, who is feigning illness, and his father David (vv. 6-7); the third is the violent encounter between Amnon and Tamar (vv. 8-18); and lastly, the fourth scene is when Absalom meets the violated

Tamar, tries to calm her, and takes her into his protection (vv. 19-20). Amnon is the common denominator in all these scenes, being mentioned in all of them, but whereas in the first three—the preparation and execution of the rape—he is the active agent, in the fourth he remains in the background and the active agent is Absalom. Thus, while Absalom has a relatively brief narration time, he has a central position in the structural scheme: in the opening, in the conclusion, and in the fourth, climactic scene of the three-and-four structure. Here the three-and-four organization points up the contrast between the attitude of the brothers to Tamar: the rapacious Amnon versus the sensitive, protective Absalom.

The Patterned Scene

Another example of a repetitive structure with fixed stages is that of a mission, which is chiefly used in stories of consecration or commissioning.[40] In this model, the author generally adheres to the following regular stages: encounter, appointment, refusal, encouragement (possibly more than once), request for signs or proof, and fear. The story of the commissioning of Gideon (Judg 6:11-24) is a perfect example of this pattern, in the form of a single scene, featuring the same personae, location, and time.[41]

Without realizing the angel's identity, Gideon meets an angel of God when he is threshing wheat inside the winepress, to keep the grain safe from the raiding Midianites. The angel greets him, saying "The LORD is with you, valiant warrior!" (v. 12), to which Gideon replies doubtfully, "Please, my lord, if the LORD is with us, why has all this befallen us? Where are all His wondrous deeds about which our fathers told us, 'Truly the LORD brought us up from Egypt?' Now the LORD has abandoned us and delivered us into the hands of Midian" (v. 13; the encounter: vv. 11-13). The angel hears and nominates Gideon, saying: "Go in this strength of

yours and deliver Israel from the Midianites. I herewith make you
My messenger" (v. 14; the commissioning). Gideon refuses, arguing
that his clan is the humblest in Manasseh and he is the youngest
in his father's house (v. 15; the refusal). The angel encourages
Gideon, saying, "I will be with you, and you shall defeat Midian
to a man" (v. 16; the encouragement). Gideon, beginning to suspect that his interlocutor is an angel, asks for a sign and even suggests what it should be. The angel gives Gideon a series of proofs,
at the end of which he vanishes in the fire (vv. 17-21; the request
for signs or proof). Gideon, realizing that he has encountered an
angel of God, is alarmed and fears that he is doomed to die
because he has seen an angel face to face (v. 22; the fear). At this
point he is given further encouragement: "Have no fear, you shall
not die" (v. 23; another encouragement). The story ends with the
building of an altar on the site of the revelation, which became
a sacred site. The use of the pattern of mission, a familiar one
in biblical literature, indicates Gideon's status as God's elect.
Here the pattern is used to emphasize that Gideon was appointed
by God.

Other stories of consecration may contain the same motifs,
though not necessarily in the same order. For example, the story
of the election of Moses to lead the exodus presents him as a
unique leader, unlike any other (Exod 3:1-4:17). In this story, the
encounter takes the form of God's appearance to Moses in a burn-
ing bush (3:2-6a), followed by the stage of fear, and only afterwards comes the appointment or election (3:7-10). Moses hears
that the purpose of his mission is to go to Pharaoh and bring the
Israelites out of Egypt, and he at once refuses: "Who am I that I
should go to Pharaoh and free the Israelites from Egypt?" (3:11).
He is given encouragement but continues to resist and demand
further signs, such as: "When I come to the Israelites and say to
them, 'The God of your fathers has sent me to you,' and they ask
me, 'What is his name?' what shall I say to them?" (3:13). When
God tells him the name, Moses says, "What if they do not believe

me and do not listen to me, but say: 'The LORD did not appear to you!'" (4:1). Then God gives him three signs that he can perform before the people: the staff that turns into a snake, his hand that becomes leprous and is restored, and, finally, water from the Nile that turns into blood when it is spilled upon the dry ground (4:2-9). But even after receiving these signs, Moses refuses, saying, "Please, O LORD, I have never been a man of words, either in times past or now that You have spoken to Your servant; I am slow of speech and slow of tongue" (4:10). God points out to Moses that it is He who gives a man speech and will also instruct him what to say. Yet Moses still holds back, saying, "Please, O LORD, make someone else Your agent" (4:13). This fifth refusal, after all the signs, makes God angry, and God decides to divide the mission between Moses and Aaron, though the hierarchy is clear: Moses is the one who will receive the word of God, and he will transmit it to Aaron to bring to the people. So this story of consecration contains the same motifs that we have seen in Gideon's consecration but in a different order and with a special extension of the stages of refusal, encouragement, and signs.

Evidently, even when the biblical author uses an established structure, the author feels free to adapt it to the specific story. Therefore, when the author comes to describe Moses, the greatest of Israelite leaders and the one who carries out the hardest mission in the people's history, the author stresses Moses' unwillingness to undertake the mission and his awareness of the immense responsibility—the greater the mission, the greater the responsibility, and consequently the greater the resistance to it. In the case of the unique leader Moses, this gives rise to the special structure of his story of consecration. The deviations from the pattern serve special functions.

≈⁾

We have seen that in constructing the plots the biblical author uses various structural models, of which I have noted several examples. The author does not spell out which structure has been chosen, and it is up to the readers to discover if the choice of one model over another contributes to the integrity of the whole work. Did the author prefer "showing" over "telling," or vice versa, and why? Did the author choose to use the three-and-four structure, and to what advantage? Will an analysis of the scene units reveal a symmetry, and what does the story gain by it? Which stage contains the change, and why? Certainly, when we realize that there is a connection between the structure and the particular content the author chooses to emphasize—in other words, that the decision to organize the plot with all its units in such-and-such a structure is a functional decision—this ensures that we do not ignore the structure when following the plot.

So far we have examined some plot structures but not without reference to the dramatis personae. Therefore, the next chapter will focus on characters.

Six

Creating Characters with Minimal Means

It is a truism that there can be no event without a character, just as there cannot be a character in a story to whom
nothing at all happens, either outwardly or inwardly. The
character may activate the event, or vice versa—come into
being through it. When the character needs the event so as
to fulfill himself or herself, not only action is required but
also other characters, whether active or activated. (199)
—Josef Ewen, *Character in Narrative*

HERMANN GUNKEL WAS THE FIRST SCHOLAR to pay attention to
the distinctive way that characters are depicted in biblical stories.
In the introduction to his commentary on *Genesis,* where he deals
with the literary form of the legends, he writes:

This economy of the legends is remarkable to us. After all,
we are accustomed to encountering skillfully portrayed
characterizations consisting of many individual elements in

modern literary works. This skill of the ancient narrators
differs significantly. Of course, it depends on the actual circumstances of the ancient period since people of that time
were simpler than complicated people now. (1997:xxxii)

According to Gunkel, the form of the legends in the Book of
Genesis "indicates the poverty of this old art" (xxx). He connects
this poverty with "the limited ability to comprehend" (xxx). On
the other hand, "this very poverty has its special advantage. The
limited scope within which the narrator must operate forced him
to apply his whole artistic power to the most minor points. These
creations are as concentrated and as effective as they are brief"
(xxx). As a result, "The legend narrator, furthermore, did not
expect his hearers—as the modern novelist can—to attend to
many persons simultaneously" (xxx). Gunkel finds in Genesis "a
particular folk psychology" that "was unable to comprehend and
portray many, and certainly not all, of the aspects of a person"
(xxxii). He is not struck either by the fact that "the narrators econ-
omize remarkably in their descriptions of the person's outward
appearance" (xxxiv), nor that there are "so few statements concerning the psychic life of the heroes" (xxxiv). He does admit the existence of more developed forms, using less minimal means, which
can be found in story-cycles, such as the stories of Joseph or in
2 Samuel, which he describes as "mature art" (xxxii). Seeking to
understand the main reason for using minimal means, he draws
the following conclusion: "Thus, one can clearly discern the
esthetic interest of the narrators. For them, action is primary; characterization is only secondary" (xxxiv), or in other words: "the old
legends subjugate everything to the action. Other literatures have
accounts in which the action is only the framework or the link, but
the key is the psychological portrait, the ingenious conversation, or
the idea. These ancient Hebrew legends differ entirely. Above all
else, the ancient required action from the narrator" (xxxix).
    There is no mistaking the ambivalence in Gunkel's statements.
He describes the inferiority of the ancient Hebrew story while at

the same time noting the advantage of minimization. He contrasts the frugal form of the ancient legends with "maturer art." We should recall that Aristotle considered plot as "the basic principle, the heart and soul, as it were, of tragedy" (*Poetics* 6.37–38). In light of modern theories of literature, we know that the creation of characters with the bare means of the short action story is no less sophisticated than the work of authors who dwell upon the mental life.[1]

This ability to create characters with spare means and many gaps, which nevertheless give the impression of depth and complexity, was called by Robert Alter, a critic of comparative literature, "the art of reticence." At the end of a chapter devoted to characterization, he states:

> The Greek tendency to narrative specification, as I suggested earlier, seems to be one that modern literary practice has by and large adopted and developed. Precisely for that reason, we have to readjust our habits as readers in order to bring an adequate attentiveness to the rather different narrative maneuvers that are characteristic of the Hebrew Bible. But the underlying biblical conception of character as often unpredictable, in some ways impenetrable, constantly emerging from and slipping back into a penumbra of ambiguity, in fact has greater affinity with dominant modern notions than do the habits of conceiving character typical of the Greek epics. (1981:129)

Classification of Characters

We open our discussion of characters and the way they are crafted by categorizing them using a method pioneered by E. M. Forster (1949:65–75). Observing the variety of literary characters, Forster distinguished between those that are "flat" and those that are "round." The flat ones, in their purest form, are built around an

? flat - Vashti

Round: Esther, Ruth

? Naomi ?

idea, or a single notion, and have no inner life, while the round characters are complex, self-aware, and capable of development and change. This division has been further refined by Josef Ewen in *Character in Narrative*. Ewen argued that between the two extremes, the flat and the rounded, there are many intermediate gradations, for example, the type-character who as well as other features has a dominant quality (1980:33–44).

Applying these methods to the female characters in the life of David, Adele Berlin (1983) shows how different kinds of women relate to the stages of his life (23–33). According to her, Michal can be defined as a developing figure, who changes from a loyal and loving wife to a bitter, contemptuous woman.[2] Berlin regards Abigail as the stereotypical "perfect wife," both intelligent and beautiful.[3] However, both Bathsheba (in 2 Samuel 11–12) and Abishag are flat characters, not important in themselves, and whose only function is to serve the plot. Therefore, she calls them "agents." Berlin also shows that the women actually represent the phases of David's private and public life.[4] David chose the loving Michal as a political instrument to advance his position in the court of her father, Saul. Once Michal realized this, she despised David and became embittered. Abigail, a woman of practical character, met David's urgent needs when he was in flight from Saul. Bathsheba, who was taken from Uriah the Hittite, represents the period of expansion of David's kingdom, when he sought to acquire more territories. Finally, Abishag, who belongs to his old age, symbolizes the senescent David, who was no longer able to control his kingdom. Thus the passage from woman to woman reflects the historical phases of David's reign.

This classification into three categories—the agents, who are subordinate to the plot; the types, who have a limited and stereotyped range of traits; and the characters, who have a broader range of traits and whose development we can observe—may be found in the biblical depiction of the patriarchs in the Book of Genesis. Abraham is a type and represents the messenger of a new religion.

He is the perfect servant of God. Although he sometimes shows a human weakness, such as fear (for example, when he pretends that his wife is his sister [Gen 12:11-13; 20:2, 11-12]), in the long run he is unfailingly obedient. Despairing of God's promise of offspring, he does not hesitate to express his doubts and to ask, "Since you have granted me no offspring, my steward shall be my heir" (Gen 15:3). His acceptance of God's promise impresses God; as the narrator says, "And because he put his trust in the LORD, He reckoned it to his merit" (v. 6). He presumes to criticize his God on the eve of the destruction of Sodom and Gomorrah: "Will you sweep away the innocent along with the guilty?" and "Far be it from you! Shall not the judge of all the earth deal justly?" (18:23, 25). On the other hand, he does not protest against God's command to sacrifice his son. Isaac is cast as a subordinate character, chiefly to serve as a transition from Abraham to Jacob, whereas Jacob, who more than any of the patriarchs represents the people of Israel, is a developing figure. Jacob changes from a young man, his mother's favorite, who would do anything to obtain the primogeniture (25:28-34; 27:1-28), to an aged patriarch, stricken and afflicted, who wishes to go down in mourning to his son in the underworld, the Sheol (37:35).

I cannot help wondering where in this classification does the figure of God belong, since God appears in most biblical stories? Is God a developing character or a type, or even a flat character?[5] Clearly, God is not a developing character, although various stories reflect God's many aspects.[6] Unlike mythology, biblical monotheism distances the deity from the sphere of other gods and sometimes even from the human sphere, avoids describing God, and does not pretend to know God well. As a result, God is depicted stereotypically as a type in most of the stories, being at times cantankerous, vindictive, forgiving, and merciful but always right and just in every situation. God is sometimes even a flat character who serves only the needs of the plot. For example, in the story of Joseph, God is always behind the scenes, ensuring

Joseph's success: "The LORD was with him and whatever he did the LORD made successful" (Gen 39:23; compare with vv. 3-5). In other words, the author is illustrating the following concept: "Many designs are in a man's mind, but it is the LORD's plan that is accomplished" (Prov 19:21). The human protagonists undergo experiences and develop and change, while God watches from above and pulls the strings.

In summary, biblical literature utilizes the gamut of character categories. The reader must not only sort them out but also examine when and why the author chooses to depict a person as developing character or as a type, and when and why the author chooses the flat option.

Characterization

Literary characterization, in the Bible as elsewhere, is achieved by a variety of means that are usually labeled "direct" or "indirect."[7] Direct characterization is provided by the narrator or by one of the persons in the story, while indirect characterization is the product of an analysis of the persona's discourse and his/her actions and conduct.

The following passage is an example of direct characterization by the narrator: "The man's name was Nabal, and his wife's name was Abigail. The woman was intelligent and beautiful, but the man, a Calebite, was a hard man and an evildoer" (1 Sam 25:3). The narrator himself informs us about Abigail's intelligence and Nabal's hard and evil character and, because—as we shall see in chapter 7—we do not doubt or question the biblical narrator's statements, the characterization is assumed by the reader to be reliable. Thus, by using reliable narrators, biblical authors transmit their various intentions. The question remains: How should direct characterizations communicated by another figure be regarded? For example, Abigail describes her husband to David thus: "Please, my lord, pay no attention to the wretched fellow Nabal. For he is just what his name says: His name means 'boor' and he is a boor" (v. 25). This is direct characterization, but we may question its reliability. Abigail may have had an interest in depicting her husband in this light in order to appeal to David, either because she was trying to save her family's property or because she was nursing long-term hopes about David. In this specific case, the possibility of doubting Abigail's words is rejected because her description corresponds to the narrator's, and if the latter's statement is considered reliable, so must be the statement of a character that matches it.

However, the fact that a direct statement could be unreliable is one of the reasons that led Alter to propose a scale of characterization that he described as a "scale of means, in ascending order of explicitness and certainty, for conveying information about the motives, the attitudes, the moral nature of characters" (1981:116). This scale ranges from the lowest level, which is "in the realm of inference," via the middle categories, which are the "weighing of claims" and "relative certainty," to the highest level, which is "the reliable narrator's explicit statement" (117).

The lowest level is the attempt to characterize the figure through his or her conduct or external appearance. For example, what can we deduce about the personality of Moses from the episode in which Moses kills an Egyptian for beating one of his Hebrew brethren and then buries the Egyptian's body in the sand (Exod 2:11-12)? Does this act demonstrate Moses' moral fiber? His sense of justice? Or that he was hasty and hot-headed? Perhaps he had the personality of a fanatical nationalist.[8] What can we deduce about Nabal the Carmelite's character from the fact that he refused to pay money to a band of outlaws who claimed that they had guarded his flocks though he had not asked them to do so (1 Sam 25:10-11)? Or what can we deduce about the character of Absalom's sister Tamar from the information that she was

beautiful (2 Sam 13:1)? Does it mean that she was a proud type?
Or that she was a seductress? The figure's actions and external
description serve as the basis for speculation that must be
verified or disproved by means of other information supplied by
the story.

The middle level is the balancing of arguments. When we compare Nabal's statement—"Who is David? Who is the son of Jesse?
There are many slaves nowadays who run away from their mas-
ters" (1 Sam 25:10)—with what David's men say on his behalf
about the protection they had given Nabal's shepherds (v. 7), the
question arises: Who is telling the truth? But when we compare
these statements with what Nabal's servant said to Abigail—
namely, that David and his men had indeed protected Nabal's
flock from all harm (vv. 14-16)—it strengthens the impression that
Nabal's statement is untrustworthy, and that he is simply unwilling to pay. This supposition is further strengthened when David
proposes that Nabal ask his men if he is telling the truth
(v. 8) and the servant speaks to Abigail and confirms everything
David says in the same words (vv. 7, 15). The process of balancing
arguments consists of such comparisons and also includes the
characters' own statements, which may be motivated by different
intentions.

At the top of the scale are the narrator's explicit statements,
which in biblical stories always represent the truth. In this case the
narrator's statement that Nabal was a "hard man and an evildoer"
(v. 3) is a reason to suspect Nabal's adherence to the law and leads
to the conclusion that his refusal to pay is simply one of his usual
tricks. Thus, the careful use of the various means, from deduction
through the balancing of arguments to the narrator's statements
—and sometimes silences—enables the biblical author to endow
his personae with added depth, which is not always discernible in
a first reading.

As for the narrator's silences, such as when the narrator avoids
the explicit characterization of the protagonists, a character's traits

may be deduced indirectly. In the first conflict between Saul and Samuel (1 Sam 13:1-18), for instance, what did happen at Gilgal, after Jonathan killed the prefect of the Philistines, who then mustered in Michmas to attack Israel with "30,000 chariots and 6,000 horsemen, and troops as numerous as the sands of the seashore" (1 Sam 13:8)? The narrator contents himself with stating objective facts, such as the size of the Philistine army, while Saul's army came to only 3,000 men. Saul and his army waited for Samuel in Gilgal for seven days, as agreed, for the seer to make the burnt offering to God and instruct Saul how to act (10:8). The narrator even notes that as the Philistine army gathered, many Israelites "hid in caves, among thorns, among rocks, in tunnels, and in cisterns" (13:6), and many others crossed the Jordan to its eastern bank. During that time, while waiting for Samuel, Saul's army dwindled: "But when Samuel failed to come to Gilgal, and the people began to scatter, Saul said, 'Bring me the burnt offering and the sacrifice of well-being'; and he presented the burnt offering. He had just finished presenting the burnt offering when Samuel arrived . . ." (1 Sam 13:8-10).

This direct report by the narrator, describing the circumstances without any characterization, gives rise to many questions: Where was Samuel at this time? Why did he not come sooner? What are we to make of the timing of Samuel's arrival just when Saul finished presenting the burnt offering? Did Samuel hide somewhere and wait for Saul to finish the rite? Be that as it may, Samuel reproaches Saul and says to him, "The LORD will seek out a man after His own heart, and the LORD will appoint Him ruler over his own people, because you did not abide by what the LORD had commanded you" (v. 14). After delivering this discouraging announcement, Samuel leaves, and now the narrator reports another significant fact: "Saul numbered the troops who remained with him—about 600 strong" (v. 15). With this army he is now supposed to go to war against the Philistines and their chariots. This is a conundrum: Who is to blame for those days of inaction, with the commander waiting, not daring go to war, and in the meantime 80 percent of the troops slipping away? Is it Saul, who perhaps did not obey the order exactly, or the seer, who allowed the situation to deteriorate to such as extent? What can we learn about the character of these two personae? There is no direct characterization. The narrator contents himself with facts and gaps or mystifying silences. Deducing these facts prevents us from regarding Saul simply as disobedient to Samuel or regarding Samuel as merely the messenger who conveys God's words. It leads us to consider the critical circumstances, to wonder about the seer's behavior, and to understand Saul and even to identify with him in this predicament.[9] The narrator's silence, then, does not deprive his characters of complexity and depth; indeed, it involves the reader's independent consideration, which sometimes produces unexpected results.

Another example of the narrator's avoidance of direct means is the story of David's response to the news of the death of Saul and his sons (2 Sam 1:1-16). After Saul and his sons fell on Mount Gilboa, a young Amalekite arrived at David's camp and reported to him what had happened on the battlefield, and even admitted that he had killed Saul at his request and as proof produced the king's crown and armlet. However, the young man's story is full of ambiguities. Replying to David's question, "How do you know that Saul and his son Jonathan are dead?" he says, "I happened to be at Mount Gilboa" (vv. 5-6). It seems unlikely that a person just happened to wander onto a battlefield. His description of the exchange between him and Saul is also suspicious: "I saw Saul leaning on his spear and the chariots and horsemen closing in on him" (v. 7), when he found the time to call out to him and to ask him who he was. Moreover, being an Amalekite hardly made him worthy of the trust and the confidence of the king. Therefore, Moshe Zvi Segal, in his introduction to *The Books of Samuel*, writes:

In reality, the Amalekite was lying, and made up a story to please David. His lie is evident in his statement, "I happened to be at Mount Gilboa" (v. 6). Because in reality the Amalekite was one of a band of outlaws and robbers who used to follow armies to the battlefield and pounce on it like vultures, to strip the dead and kill the wounded in order to despoil them, and this was how the Amalekite found the fallen Saul on Mount Gilboa. Perhaps he did stab him again, to make sure he was dead, then removed his royal insignia and took them to David, hoping to receive a generous reward. And the writer repeats the words of the Amalekite, without suggesting that they are truthful.[10]

It is reasonable to assume that this particular Amalekite knew that David would be interested in the news from the battlefield, and therefore he brought the necessary proof (crown and armlet), perhaps hoping to be rewarded. David, whose intelligence is never in doubt, hears the strange report without asking questions. David does not even try to find out if the Amalekite is telling the truth but rends his clothes, as do all his men, and proceeds to fast and lament Saul and his son Jonathan and the men of Israel who have fallen. This continues until evening, when David summons the young man and conducts a curious interrogation. He asks him only one question: "Where are you from?" (2 Sam 1:13). When he hears that the young man is an Amalekite, David responds: "How did you dare to lift your hand and kill the LORD's anointed?" (v. 14). At once he orders one of his men, "Come over and strike him!" The Amalekite is struck down and dies, and David adds, "Your blood be on your own head! Your own mouth testified against you when you said, 'I put the LORD's anointed to death'" (v. 16). It is fitting that David has the Amalekite publicly take upon himself the responsibility for killing Saul, God's anointed. Having the Amalekite killed also shows David avenging Saul's death and his zeal for Saul's memory.

The narrator's silences and the absence of direct means enable us to interpret the story as follows: David did not really want to know the truth, so he did not question the messenger too closely, or he would have found that rather than the assassin of the Lord's anointed, this was merely a wretched looter, who hoped to gain something from the battle. David was content to let the Amalekite accept responsibility for Saul's death. This way he could build up his own image as the just person who avenged the king of Israel, and who, instead of having a direct interest in Saul's death, loudly laments it. How do we define David's behavior, then, as image-building or as sincere emotion? The narrator is silent and offers no unequivocal information, while providing plenty of ambiguities, gaps, and circumstantial evidence that can readily support the unconventional interpretation of image-building.[11]

Moreover, we come to know David as a master of public elegies. We are familiar with his famous lament for Saul and Jonathan (2 Sam 1:17-27), but there is also another lament, for Abner (2 Sam 3:33-34), the commander of Saul's army. After Saul and his three sons were killed, Abner became the commander of the army of Ish-bosheth, Saul's fourth son. But Abner had greater ambitions; he coveted the crown. Realizing that Ish-bosheth was not ready to give up his position, Abner decided to switch sides, join David, and persuade his people to do the same.[12] David's pact with Abner enraged Joab, the commander of David's army, because Abner had killed Joab's brother, Asahel. Consequently, Joab killed Abner. David's reaction was to rush to the "media" to inform everyone that he was not to blame: "'Both I and my kingdom are forever innocent before the LORD of shedding the blood of Abner son of Ner. May [the guilt] fall upon the head of Joab and all his father's house'" (2 Sam 3:28-29). Naturally, Abner's death was marked by solemn mourning, and the king wept before the people and composed an elegy. Again, David fasted and, when urged to eat, swore that he would not do so before sundown. Here the narrator adds the following statement: "All the troops took note of it and approved, just as all the troops approved everything else the king did. That day all the troops and all Israel knew that it was not by the king's will that Abner son of Ner was killed" (vv. 36-37). Was this genuine sorrow and a sincere lament, or was this calculated behavior by David intended to convince the people that he was not responsible for the killing, thus retaining the loyalty of Abner's followers and stopping them from going back to Ish-bosheth?

Later Ish-bosheth himself was killed. The assassins brought his head to David, who sentenced them to death and hastened to declare, "The man who told me in Ziklag that Saul was dead thought he was bringing good news. But instead of rewarding him for the news I seized and killed him. . . . I will certainly avenge [Ish-bosheth's] blood on you, and I will rid the earth of you" (2 Sam 4:10-11). David's behavior can be described as a systematic repetitive pattern, which shows clearly that what mattered above all to David was his image and how he appeared in the eyes of the people. He does not need spin-doctors, since he comes across every screen, even that of history as shown by the commentaries that describe him as "grieving profoundly and sincerely" (Bar-Efrat 1996b:10, 33, 45), without even allowing that his feelings could have been mixed and complex.[13]

Only a master storyteller could maneuver so well between the image of the leader, supposedly just and compassionate, who recoils in horror from the "savage sons of Zeruiah," and the sophisticated, astute, brazen personality with a brilliant gift for public relations. Without a doubt, in this analysis, David is flawed but very human and quick to see every avenue to power.

This characterization of David is achieved by indirect means through the reader's deductions and conclusions. Consequently, some readers are impressed by David's sensitivity and morality, while others are impressed by his cleverness and single-minded ambition for the crown. By using an indirect approach, the narrator achieves a level of ambiguity that he may have wished for in depicting this complex character. Such ambiguity is described by Erich Auerbach as "background": "The human beings in the biblical stories have greater depths of time, fate, and consciousness than do the human beings in Homer . . . their thoughts and feelings have more layers, are more entangled" (1957:9). It is worth noting that Auerbach also interprets the representation of God in this way.

Creating a complex character in a series of stories is easier than creating one in a single short tale. The complex characters that we have seen, Saul, David, and Joseph, each appear in cycles of stories. The more chainlike the cycle—with a system of cause and effect and with every story linked to its predecessor—the better the gradual formation of the character. But when the cycle is eclectic (for example, the stories of Abraham, or the stories of the exodus from Egypt), the character ends up as the sum of the qualities that the author wishes to highlight, as indeed do Abraham and Moses.

In the above discussion we noted three kinds of characters in the biblical story: types, subordinate figures ("flat"), and complex or developing figures ("round"). The first two are common in religious or didactic literature, where their function is to help communicate an unequivocal and purposeful message. Why then does biblical literature, which is religious literature with a didactic purpose, include complex characters? In other words, what was the idea behind the creation of developing characters?

The Character of God and Its Implication for Human Characters

The answer to the above question—it seems to me—must be sought in the intellectual and theological world of biblical literature and its ideological struggles.[14] The need to promote the idea of a remote deity, in which the shrine is the dwelling place not of the deity itself but of its name, calls for new considerations even in the sphere of stories.[15] If God remains in heaven, God must be taken off the list of personae on stage. Thus, stories were created in which God is generally behind the scenes and intervenes only in indirect ways, such as through dreams or through the prophets. I do not maintain that this is true throughout the biblical stories.[16] I do argue, however, that those stories in which God is behind the scenes reflect the desire for a deity that cannot be depicted and as much as possible to avoid attributing flesh-and-blood qualities to Him. God's position in these stories is affected by two differing perceptions of God's management style of the world: intervening or observing; among us or above us; and acting or only supervising. The more anthropomorphic and concrete the concept, the more God is seen as intervening, being among us, and acting. On the other hand, the greater God's distance from the human sphere and flesh-and-blood terms, the more God is projected as an observing deity who only supervises events. God's portrayal differs greatly from one story to the next. For example, the stories of the beginnings of humankind, in which God takes part (Genesis 1–11) contrasts with the story of Joseph (Genesis 37–50), in which God is only mentioned by the narrator and the acting personae. The story of the exodus and the wandering in the desert (Exodus and Numbers) stresses the presence of God in the Israelite camp, which is quite different from the story of the succession to the throne where the prophet Nathan acts as God's emissary (2 Samuel 9–20 and 1 Kings 1–2). In the stories of the Book of Judges, in which God or God's Spirit takes part in the deliverance is set against the Book of Ruth. Finally, the Book of Chronicles actually describes the appearance of God in the temple (2 Chron 7:1-4), but in the Book of Esther, God is not mentioned once.

As these examples show, the choice of depicting God as more or less intervening is not a matter of earlier or later stories. The late Book of Chronicles opts for a concrete concept of the deity while the earlier books, like Samuel and Kings, prefer the remote and less concrete image. Therefore, the depiction of God is a question of a conceptual, philosophical preference. The less concrete idea of God was an option not a norm, and authors could choose the form that suited their own worldviews and intentions. One way or the other, the decision whether to involve God in the story or distance God from the action had an immediate effect on the world of the story. The more God is seen as commanding and reproving, punishing or merciful, the more the human characters are depicted as flat characters or as singular types such rebellious, sinful, or obedient. When God is portrayed as distant, there seems to be greater scope, or living space, for human motives and their complexities. In the story of the Garden of Eden (Gen 2:4b—3:24), God walks about "at the breezy time of day" (2:8); inspires awe; punishes Adam and Eve by clothing them in "garments of skins" (3:21); consults the angels, and installs the cherubim with "the fiery ever-turning sword" (3:24) to guard the way to the tree of life. Meanwhile, Adam and Eve are depicted as types of sinners. By contrast, in the succession narrative (2 Samuel 9–20 and 1 Kings 1–2), events occur because people cause them, being impelled by their personalities, ambitions, and lusts, as well as by apparently unexpected circumstances or by economic, political, and social forces. At the same time, there are ways to underline the role of distant divine providence, notably with the use of prophets, who are special emissaries mediating between God and humans. David is punished for his sins by a prophet sent by God to reprove him. Even an unforeseen occurrence, like Amnon's rape of Tamar, is found to be part of the chastisement of David.

A story-world in which the deity appears as an acting figure is not subject to the laws of everyday reality and is therefore replete with wonders and miracles. Whereas a story-world in which the deity is out of sight and remote is a more reasonable world, the behavior of the characters is comprehensible, so that there is scope for a life of the mind, for psychological considerations and the like, which allows the readers to follow the characters and their development. For example, David starts out as an ambitious young man with aspirations to the throne and ends up by being indifferent to the affairs of state. And Saul initially has no interest in ruling yet grows to be obsessed with power. In the Book of Chronicles, by contrast, personalities are not complex: David appears as the type who founds kingdoms and lays the groundwork for the future, while Solomon is depicted as one who carries out his father's testament and builds a temple. Both characters are portrayed as obedient to the will of God.

The figure of Samson belongs to the type of deliverer alongside an intervening deity and demonstrates how biblical literature depicts a hero who no longer belongs to the mythical or epic tradition but is a kind of Israelite Hercules. He is a hero in the service of the one God, the exclusive source of power (Judges 13–16).[17] In this type of story the author chooses to open with a barren woman giving birth in miraculous circumstances—a typical way of emphasizing divine intervention (Judg 13:2-24). Samson is depicted as a hero who depends on the spirit of the Lord, which either grips him (14:6, 19; 15:14) or moves him (13:25), and woe to him when it fails him (16:19-21). His hair is not the magic source of his strength but a sign of his special position in relation to God, that of a Nazirite (13:5; 16:17). Furthermore, Samson has no extraordinary dimensions; he is a hero who prays, and his prayers reveal his dependence upon God. At Lehi, after killing one thousand Philistines and feeling thirsty, he appeals to God saying, "You Yourself have granted this great victory through Your servant; and must I now die of thirst and fall into the hands of the uncircumcised?" (15:18). At the end of his life, when the Philistines bring him to the temple of Dagon to entertain them, he calls to God: "Oh Lord God! Please remember me, and give me strength just this once, O God, to take revenge of the Philistines, if only for one of my two eyes" (16:28).[18]

Unlike Samson, the characterization of Gideon shows two distinct personalities, with the difference based on God's perceived presence or distance. The cycle of Gideon's stories (Judg 6:1—8:28) can be divided into two parts.[19] In the first part (6:11—7:23), God's intervention is outstanding, while in the second part (7:24—8:27a), God remains behind the scenes.

In the first part, Gideon is a timid type. He is afraid because he has seen an angel face to face, and he needs to be reassured by God, who says, "Have no fear, you shall not die" (Judg 6:23). When he is sent to demolish his father's altar of Baal, the narrator reports that "Gideon took ten of his servants and did as the LORD had told him; but as he was afraid to do it by day, on account of his father's household and the townspeople, he did it by night" (6:27). A short time later, before the battle with the Midianites, God sends Gideon at night to attack the Midianite camp, but first God reassures him: "And if you are afraid to attack, first go down to the camp with your attendant Purah and listen to what they say; after that you will have the courage to attack the camp" (7:10-11). And the fearful Gideon does go there with his attendant Purah. This part of the cycle is full of signs whose purpose is to give Gideon strength and assure him that God is with him. This continues until he witnesses God's deliverance and the flight of the Midianites.

In the second part of the cycle, Gideon's personality changes radically. Suddenly he is a charismatic leader who uses diplomatic tactics in dealing with the men of Ephraim, saying, "Ephraim's gleanings are better than Abiezer's vintage!" (8:2). Gideon metes out harsh punishment to the towns of Succoth and Penuel, which had failed to support him in the chase after the Midianites (8:4-21). In this part, God is behind the scenes and Gideon changes from timid deliverer to decisive leader.

The editorial decision to divide the units of the Gideon cycle into two different sections is related to the two editorial guidelines in the Book of Judges, namely, signs and leadership. God communicates with his people by means of signs, but the people are focused on the continuing rule of a central human leader. The two sets of stories in the Gideon cycle are organized according to these guidelines, with the first dedicated to the signs of God, and the second to human leadership. Each set thus calls for a different kind of figure. In the first set, Gideon is depicted as fearful and is given signs by the intervening God; in the second, he is a charismatic and independent leader whom the people beg to be their king: "'Rule over us—you, your son, and your grandson as well; for you have saved us from the Midianites'" (8:22). The Gideon stories clearly illustrate how the image of the deity has a direct impact on the characterization of the human personae.

Character and the Role of the Reader

One of the difficulties in understanding a character's place in the story is that we often come to biblical stories with strong preconceptions. Jezebel, for instance, is a notoriously evil figure, described as responsible for the establishment of Baal worship in northern Israel (1 Kings 16:31-33; 18:4, 19; 19:1-2). She is remembered as the one who incited Ahab to do "what was displeasing to the LORD" (21:23-26). As a result, many readers conclude that Jezebel is the leading figure in the story of Naboth's vineyard (chap. 21), and that she was responsible for the murder of Naboth.[20] Yet that story contains numerous elements that point the accusing finger at Ahab. Earlier, in our discussion of the structure of this story, we saw that out of its seven units—the opening unit, five scene units, and the conclusion—Ahab is prominently figured in six (see pp. 54–56 above). The only scene without him is the climax scene of the trial, from which Jezebel is also absent. In fact, Jezebel appears in only two scenes in the palace and is not mentioned in the opening or conclusion. In the first palace scene (21:4-10), she is acting on Ahab's behalf and uses his seal to order the staged trial, and in the second (vv. 15-16) she informs him that the order was carried out. It is Ahab who, while lying on his bed, motivates Jezebel. He does not restrain her from using his seal. The townspeople who hold the trial do so because they have received an order bearing Ahab's seal. Moreover, God, who sends Elijah to confront Ahab by saying, "Would you murder and take possession?" (v. 19), does not even mention Jezebel. Elijah's challenge is addressed to Ahab alone.[21]

There are four criteria to help us determine who is the leading character in any given work of literature: one, the focus of interest; two, quantitative; three, structural; and four, thematic.[22] When these criteria are applied, they all point to Ahab as the leading character. Regarding the focus of interest, the issue is whether Ahab will succeed in obtaining the vineyard that he is so keen on. Quantitatively, we have already seen that he is present in all but one of the scenes. Structurally, he is present in many of the strong parts of the story, especially the opening and conclusion. Finally, the central theme in the story of Ahab's guilt in the murder of Naboth is stated by God himself. Thus, the leading character in this story is Ahab, and he bears responsibility for the crime, not Jezebel, nor the townspeople, nor the scoundrels, who are all only accomplices in the king's crime.

In another example, Absalom is often criticized and depicted in pejorative terms because he killed his brother and rebelled against his father. However, a close examination of the way his character is depicted in the story of Amnon and Tamar (2 Sam 13:1-22) reveals that the author of the story of the succession did not present things simplistically but, in fact, created a complex character who begins to take shape in this earlier story. Here the prominent figures are, of course, the rapist, Amnon, and his victim, Tamar. Amnon is present in every stage of this story, from the opening, through the planning of the rape, the rape scene, the resolution, and the conclusion. In the stages of planning and the act itself, he is the active character; in the resolution, when Absalom meets Tamar, he asks her about Amnon, and in the conclusion, the narrator refers to Amnon as the one who violated Tamar. The narrator takes pains to implicate Amnon and present him in the worst possible light.[23] In chapter 4 we focused on the openings of stories, and we saw that Amnon is presented from the start as not simply loving his half-sister but as having a particular interest in her. In the planning stage, he deceives his clever friend Jonadab, who advises him to feign illness so that his father would visit him and order Tamar to make him some strengthening food. Then Amnon deceives his father, who gives Tamar the order. When Tamar has finished preparing the food and has fed him, Amnon asks her to lie with him. When she refuses, he ignores her pleas, rapes her violently, and then orders her to get out. When she begs to remain, he orders his attendant to throw her out and bar the door after her.

The story is twenty-two verses long, and eleven of these are devoted to the scene of the rape (vv. 8-18). Clearly, the author did not try to play down Amnon's physical or mental viciousness. Nor should we overlook the fact that Amnon was the heir to the throne. At the same time, we must not forget that the story opens not with Amnon but with Absalom: "Absalom son of David had a beautiful sister named Tamar" (v. 1), which points to the closeness between Absalom and Tamar. Their meeting after the rape (vv. 19-20) is evidence that this is not merely a genetic connection of having the same mother. Tamar, who has been ejected, rends her ornamented royal tunic, throws ashes on her head, and goes out crying aloud. When her brother Absalom encounters her, he asks in the gentlest way, "Was your brother Amnon with you?" (not: "Did he lie with you?").[24] He asks her to keep quiet about it for the time being because Amnon is her brother (meaning that the issue must be resolved within the family) and takes her under his protection. To calm her, he tells her not to brood over it. The conclusion also informs us that King David heard about the rape and was greatly upset but said nothing. We noted earlier (pp. 25–27) that according to the Septuagint, the Masoretic Text lacks a verse that explains the reason for the king's silence: he does not chastise his son Amnon because he loves him and because he is his first-born. In other words, the matter is not resolved within the family but suppressed. Though David, as the king, is the source of justice in the kingdom, he prefers to bury the issue and to go on as though nothing has happened. Absalom finds this situation intolerable, and the story concludes with the narrator's statement that Absalom hates Amnon because he has violated his sister Tamar. This is an extremely significant statement, because it warns us not to imagine that Absalom hates Amnon because he is the firstborn and heir to the throne but because Amnon has abused his sister.

The story that follows the rape of Tamar is the murder of Amnon by Absalom (13:23-37). The narrator emphasizes that two years had passed between the rape and the murder. This means that for two whole years Absalom waited in vain for his father to take action. His father's inaction pained Absalom greatly, which is shown by the sequel, when he has a daughter and names her Tamar, after his unfortunate sister (14:27). All this tells us that Absalom did not act hastily or arbitrarily. We may well wonder if David imagined that Tamar would remain desolate in Absalom's house for the rest of her life? Did he think that by ignoring the situation he could restore things to the way they had been before the rape, and that Amnon was good enough to rule the kingdom? Did David think that it did not matter that Absalom and Amnon did not speak? Or perhaps he ignored this, too, so long as all was quiet. This open-ended conclusion suggests that there will be a sequel.

As we take note of Absalom's conduct and his sensitivity, at this stage we would sympathize with any criticism that he cared to make against his brother or father. At the end of this story, if we were to compare Absalom, who opens and closes it, with David and Amnon, we would certainly conclude that Absalom is the better man. It therefore seems that this story communicates sympathy for Absalom and an early justification for his subsequent actions, to which other justifications are added later. By the time we come to the story of the rebellion, we can hardly overlook the cumulative effect of these justifications, which at any rate show that Absalom was bitterly and justifiably critical of his father and that his rebellion was not motivated only by a desire for power and an impatience to reach the throne.[25]

The last example is taken from the story of Judah and Tamar in Genesis 38. Many scholars maintain that it was meant to show Judah in a bad light, mainly because he had married "the daughter of a certain Canaanite whose name was Shua" (v. 2).[26] But when we look closely at the way Judah is depicted in this story, we notice a number of devices that present him in a favorable light. The opening of the story describes how Judah's first two sons, Er and Onan, died, and how Judah does not want to follow the custom and give their widow, his daughter-in-law Tamar, to the youngest son, Shelah, because he thinks that Shelah might die, too. Instead, Judah sends Tamar back to her father's house. The plot begins some years later, when Tamar decides to take matters into her hands to avoid being left unmarried. She dresses as a harlot, meets Judah, and becomes pregnant by him. When Judah hears that Tamar is pregnant, he orders her to be burned, but when he discovers the source of her pregnancy he changes his mind. Tamar gives birth to twin sons, one of whom, Perez, will be the forefather of David's dynasty.

Judah did indeed marry a Canaanite woman, but this is not viewed by the narrator as a negative act and is not condemned. The death of his first two sons is not on account of their Canaanite origin, but because they were displeasing to the Lord. The explicit statement that Er was displeasing to the Lord, and that Onan, who refused to impregnate his brother's widow, was also displeasing to the Lord, suggests that the fault lay with them and their conduct and not with their origin. Judah's refusal to give their widow to their younger brother is also explained: "[F]or he thought, 'He too might die like his brothers'" (v. 11). The reader can sympathize with Judah, who naturally, after the death of his two sons, feared for the youngest one.[27] Describing the meeting between Judah and Tamar, the narrator mentions various facts and explanations to justify Judah's conduct. Judah visits a harlot only after the end of his mourning for his wife (v. 12); he approaches Tamar believing that she is a harlot, having no inkling that he would be committing incest. Tamar had taken off her widow's garb and veiled herself, so Judah did not recognize her as his daughter-in-law. The narrator stresses this fact at the beginning of the scene (v. 14), again in the course of it (v. 15, 16), and at its end (v. 19). The narrator also states that from the moment Judah discovered that he himself had impregnated Tamar, he was never intimate with her again (v. 26).[28] Judah even recognizes that she was justified in what she did, declaring, "She is more in the right than I" (v. 26). Finally, the fact that she conceives and bears twins suggests that Providence has intervened to bring this about.

So Judah is depicted in this story as a human being who admits that he was wrong, and who deals fairly and judges justly. His reward is the birth of Perez, from whom would descend the House of David.[29] All these devices lead to the conclusion that Judah is depicted in this story in a favorable light. At least, the narrator, who protects Judah's reputation, and God, who rewards Judah, seem to think so.

These last two factors, the narrator and God—and their contribution to the reliability of what is told—will be the subject of the next chapter.

Seven

Whom to Believe?

UNTIL NOW I HAVE REFERRED TO THE NARRATOR of the biblical story with unquestioning respect, implying that whatever the narrator says must be so. The previous chapter, dealing with the favorable characterization of Judah in the Book of Genesis, concluded with the statement that the narrator, at any rate, sought to protect Judah's reputation, and God, who rewarded him, seemed to think so, too. This implies that the narrator and God are the benchmarks of reliability and of the story's verisimilitude. Now we must ask how the positions of the narrator and God's reliability affect our understanding of the story.

The biblical authors present their stories as a meaningful history from which the readers must draw a moral. They tell us that certain things happened, and it is reasonable to assume that they want us to believe them and accept them as truth. I do not propose to tackle the question of whether the events described in these stories actually took place, since such a question is either a matter of faith or of examining the texts with the tools of the discipline of history, neither of which concerns us here. My point of departure is that, by and large, the biblical author wants to be believed by the public. The "contract" between the author and the public says that the world depicted in the stories is not fictional but real, and the stories are chronicles. This is unlike many other storytellers, who construct lifelike worlds but do not expect their readers to regard them as actual reality. In a sense, the modern reader who doubts the biblical story is violating the contract and cannot be said to represent the intended public.

The biblical story-world assumes there are nonexplicit rules that say who is above suspicion and who may be misleading us, deliberately or otherwise. In this way the reader knows when the information is reliable and can be trusted, and when it needs to be tested. One may expect that God is above suspicion and trustworthy. However, since we are dealing with stories, God, too, is known to us only through the narrator's mediation.[1]

The narrator is an unnamed, abstract figure who mediates between us and the story. The narrator tells us what happened and informs us which characters are speaking, from God to the humblest servant. Playwrights often dispense with narrators, since their characters appear on stage and tell their story, and the spectators piece the information together and so construct their world. However, when we read a story we are in the hands of the narrator. The narrator may stand outside the world of the story described, or be one of the characters in it. We can imagine the external narrator as a movie director with a film crew. The director decides what is to be filmed, for how long, where, and how. He or she is the final authority, and we the viewers depend on it and on the work of the film crew. The final product reflects the director's interpretation, viewpoint, and preferences.[2] The biblical narrative writers scarcely used a participant narrator. In fact, this only occurs in parts of the Book of Deuteronomy, dictated by Moses, and in the Book of Nehemiah, in which the author tells the story from Nehemiah's viewpoint. Most biblical authors preferred— probably for a reason, as we shall see—to use an authoritative external narrator who is above the characters. The narrator may be a prolific reporter or may withdraw and yield the floor to the characters, but even then the narrator remains inseparable from the story-world by continually reporting who the speakers are. Now and then we are reminded of the narrator's existence, with such phrases as "in those days" and "then," which confirm that the events described happened in the past and that there is a chronological gap between the narrator's time and the time of the event described. And it is the narrator, of course, who tells us what God said, or did, or even thought. Thus, the narrator tells us that "God began to create heaven and earth" (Gen 1:1), as well as that "the LORD regretted that He had made man on earth, and His heart was saddened. . . ." (Gen 6:6). Doubting the narrator of the Pentateuch, for example, means doubting the Pentateuch's authority and its laws, which is tantamount to breaking the contract.

Literary studies tends to refer to the narrator in religious terminology, such as omniscient and omnipotent, because the narrator is traditionally considered the ultimate authority in the story-world. The narrator knows all there is to know about the world of the story—even the secret thoughts and feelings of the characters, including God. Therefore, in a biblical story, God is to be trusted for reasons of faith, and the narrator is to be trusted, in this respect, as above God and as the source of the report about God. Both God and the narrator must be trustworthy and hence are the benchmark of trustworthiness for all other personae. Whatever accords with the narrator's statements or God's must be beyond doubt.

For example, the narrator quotes God's command to the man: "And the LORD God commanded the man, saying, 'Of every tree of the garden you are free to eat; but as for the tree of knowledge of good and bad, you must not eat of it; for as soon as you eat of it, you shall die'" (Gen 2:16-17). This wording offers at least two possible interpretations for this command: one, you shall die on the day you eat of it; and two, from the day you eat of it, you shall live under a sentence of death. Either way, the two possibilities threaten with death.[3] Now the serpent, being "the shrewdest of all the wild beasts" (3:1) and seeking to entice the woman, addresses her with a provocative remark that misquotes God's command but induces her to talk to him: "Did God really say: You shall not eat of any tree of the garden?" (3:1). The serpent has not finished speaking before the woman breaks in and quotes the divine command, though she could not have heard it herself, since it was given before she was created. Evidently she knows that eating the fruit of this particular tree means death. But the serpent goes on, "You are not going to die, but God knows that as soon as you eat of it your eyes will be opened and you will be like divine beings who know good and bad" (3:4-5). The serpent's speech is both truthful and misleading. The truth is that eating of that tree would make the man and the woman open their eyes and become aware of themselves and the world around them. We know this to be the truth both because this is what happened in the story, and because God says as much when he expels them from the garden: "Now that the man has become like one of us, knowing good and bad, what if he should stretch out his hand and take also from the tree of life and eat, and live forever!" (3:22). Yet the first part of the serpent's speech can be regarded as misleading or an outright lie. Perhaps when he said, "You are not going to die," he meant that they would not be mortal—which was a lie; or he may have meant that they would not die as soon as they ate the fruit. One way or the other, his quibbling statement, which justifies his description as the "shrewdest of all the wild beasts," could have been interpreted as disputing the divine command and as suggesting that God had uttered a false threat in order to frighten the man, because God feared the man's awakening reason.

We can see that the word of God and of the narrator form the criteria of credibility, while the speech of any other figure must be evaluated, either by comparison or by analysis. It is the narrator who tells us, in 2 Samuel 31, about the death of Saul and his sons on Mount Gilboa. There is no mention of the Amalekite youth in that story, which does not necessarily mean that he was not there. The narrator is omniscient but does not report everything. The narrator chooses what to tell and when. In the story of the death of Saul the narrator describes how, on the day after the battle, the Philistines came to strip the fallen soldiers, found Saul and his sons, cut off Saul's head, and stripped Saul of his armor. However, the narrator does not mention the Amalekite. Yet when the Amalekite youth arrives at David's camp he brings unmistakable proof of having been on the battlefield, the king's crown and bracelet. The Philistines had carried away the king's weapons, but the Amalekite took the royal insignia. According to the rule that the narrator is omniscient but may not tell everything, we may regard the two stories as mutually complementary. We assume that the narrator added in the second story, concerning the Amalekite youth, what was purposefully omitted in the first, which shows the narrator's power concerning what and when to reveal key information. In any event, the proof produced by the Amalekite make his story sufficiently convincing, and many commentators regard him as credible.

From Josephus in *Jewish Antiquities* to present-day biblical scholars, it has been widely accepted that the Amalekite told the truth.[4] On the other hand, as we have seen, a careful examination of the Amalekite youth's story is puzzling and may mean that it is not entirely truthful. If this is the case, then the picture changes and casts David in an unflattering light. It is noteworthy that here the narrator's silence and lack of comment on the youth's story and on David's action permits both interpretations.

The issue becomes more problematic when we compare these two versions of Saul's death with the one in the Book of Chronicles (1 Chronicles 10). I leave out the many differences between them, but here is the conclusion of the story in Chronicles, told entirely by the narrator and as such supposedly entirely credible (though there is no hint of this in the parallel story in the Book of Samuel): "Saul died for the trespass that he had committed

against the LORD in not having fulfilled the command of the
LORD; moreover, he had consulted a ghost to seek advice, and did
not seek advice of the Lord; so He had him slain and the kingdom
transferred to David son of Jesse" (1 Chron 10:13-14).[5] According
to the narrator of the Book of Chronicles, then, Saul died because
of his trespass against the LORD—in Hebrew the root of the verb
meaning "trespass" is *mʿl*. This root is used elsewhere in Chronicles in connection with a violation of a proscription, in reference
to Achar, "the troubler of Israel" (1 Chron 2:7), who is actually
Achan, whose full story is found in the Book of Joshua (chap. 7).[6]
Therefore the accusation that Saul committed a *maʿal* seems to be
a reference to his war against the Amalekites, when he failed to
wipe out their flocks. The allusion to Achan also implies that to
the author of Chronicles, Saul was a "troubler of Israel." Another
reason for Saul's death, according to this author's wording, was
that Saul did not fulfill God's command, which refers to the first
dispute between Saul and Samuel (1 Samuel 13). Samuel was angry
with Saul when he did not wait for him in Gilgal for seven days,
as agreed, but made the burnt offering himself; the reference is
suggested by the verb *šmr*—to fulfill, keep, or abide the commandments—used twice by Samuel when he reproached Saul on
that occasion (1 Sam 13:13-14). The author of Chronicles further
blackens Saul's sins by having the narrator say explicitly that "he
had consulted a ghost to seek advice, and did not seek advice of
the LORD" (1 Chron 10:13b-14a). Here the chronicler has an
opposed version—in 1 Samuel it is emphasized that Saul went to
consult the ghost only after he had despaired of consulting God:
"And Saul inquired of the LORD, but the LORD did not answer
him, either by dreams or by Urim or by prophets" (1 Sam 28:6).
So, according to the narrator of the Book of Samuel, Saul consults
the ghost only when left with no other choice, a fact stressed at the
beginning of this story, which says that it was Saul who "had forbidden [recourse to] ghosts and familiar spirits in the land" (28:3b).

The discrepancy between the narratives in Samuel and Chronicles is therefore a disagreement between two trustworthy narrators. But if both are trustworthy, how is it possible that their stories disagree? Whom should we believe?

The differences between the story in 1 Samuel 31 and that of the Amalekite youth (2 Sam 1:4b-10) is easily explained: The first report, given by the narrator, is reliable, and the second, told by one of the personae, the Amalekite, is not reliable. But this solution cannot be applied to the discordance between the narratives in Samuel and Chronicles, because in both cases the stories are told by the reliable narrator. So the question remains: whom do we believe? To this question I give a seemingly impossible answer: we should believe both of them. These two stories were written by two authors. The author of the Book of Samuel regards Saul with the respect due a king of Israel and depicts his death as heroic. To make it persuasive, the author delivers the story through the authoritative, reliable narrator. In contrast, the author of the Book of Chronicles, who is a supporter of the house of David and wants to emphasize that the monarchy was justly transferred from the house of Saul to that of David, does everything to blacken Saul's character and depict him as a great sinner. And since this author also seeks to convince the readers, the story is told through the always trustworthy narrator. Here, then, are two authors with opposing intentions, each with their own truth. The authors then and not the narrators are the source of the contradiction. As for the question about which of the two stories is historically more reliable, this is a matter for historians. For our purpose, even if it is determined that the Book of Chronicles is not a sound historical source, this does not diminish the trustworthiness of the narrator as such. The author of Chronicles, with his rhetorical approach, chooses the effective poetic option of a reliable and authoritative narrator for the world of the story for which he is responsible.

> → Narrator is distinct from author

So far we have seen that the narrator and God are always believable; now we must consider if there are any human personae in the biblical stories whom the reader may also trust implicitly. As God's emissaries and representatives, the prophets must be seen as wholly trustworthy. This, however, is not always the case. As we read through biblical narratives, we find some prophets who do not convey God's word exactly, as illustrated by an example from 1 Samuel 15.

After Saul's war with the Amalekites, when he failed to obey God's command to destroy them and everything belonging to them, God regretted that he had chosen Saul to be king of Israel: "The word of the Lord then came to Samuel: 'I regret that I made Saul king, for he has turned away from Me and has not carried out My command'" (1 Sam 15:10-11). The reader cannot doubt this statement, since God says it. The story ends with the narrator's statement, which corresponds to that of God, "the Lord regretted that He had made Saul king over Israel" (v. 35). Such close agreement between the words of God and the narrator's report means that they are infallible. Yet, in the course of the story, when Samuel reproves Saul, the latter begs the prophet to forgive his offense and to go back with him. Samuel repeats, "I will not go back with you; for you have rejected the Lord's command, and the Lord has rejected you as king over Israel" (v. 26). Then, as Samuel turns to leave, Saul seizes his coat in an attempt to convince him to stay, and it tears. Samuel regards this as symbolic of the imminent tearing of Saul's kingship: "The Lord has this day torn the kingship over Israel from you and has given it to another who is worthier than you. Moreover, the Glory of Israel does not deceive or change His mind, for He is not human that He should change His mind" (vv. 28-29). How can Samuel state that God does not change his mind, when God told him directly and explicitly that he regretted making Saul king? (In the Hebrew, the same verb, *nḥm*, is used in both statements.)

The reader, coming across these three statements, spoken by God, by the prophet, and by the narrator, must choose which of them to believe.[7] Surely we must believe the word of God, which is matched by the narrator's statement, namely, that God does and did regret what he had done. But this raises the question, how reliable is the prophet who is God's emissary? Samuel proceeds to describe God in singular terms that emphasize the difference between Him and human beings—specifically, that God does not change his mind, even though this contradicts the statements made by God himself and by the narrator. Moreover, deciding that the prophet is not to be trusted in this case can have wider implications. It may cast doubt not only about the particular case of Samuel's attitude to Saul but also about statements made by prophets elsewhere in the Bible. As we go on reading, we find in 1 Kings 13:11-19 a prophet who lies in God's name.

Returning to our story, we can only speculate about why Samuel deviated from God's word, and indeed there are any number of speculations in the commentaries on this passage. Possibly Samuel meant to say that God did not regret his decision to remove the kingship from Saul, but being furious with Saul, he went on to say that unlike men, God did not change his mind, thus speaking his own mind rather than God's. The simple conclusion from this story is that even a prophet may not always be totally reliable. Such a conclusion accords with the world of biblical beliefs and views, which stresses the difference between the human and the divine. Human beings have failings and cannot be compared with the deity, which is why biblical stories are replete with sinful kings and even depict prophets who deviate from their mission. Readers of the biblical stories must therefore keep reminding themselves that God and the narrator are always to be believed, whereas the speech of the characters in the story, even if they are God's emissaries, must be checked.

Finally, the narrator of a biblical story, like any other literary narrator, is a mediating element, chosen and fashioned by the author. The author decides how much the narrator knows, how the narrator views the events described, how these events are evaluated, if the narrator will be content with external descriptions or describe the minds of the personae, and so on. It is also the author who chooses to use a trustworthy narrator. Therefore, an attempt to understand the world of the narrator is, in effect, a glimpse into the author's world.

Eight

The Biblical Story
and the Use of Time

A STORY IS AN ART FORM THAT USES TIME. This chapter examines
some ways that authors of biblical stories manipulated time.

The German author and scholar Gotthold Ephraim Lessing
(1729–1781), in his famous work *Laocoon* (also known as *An Essay
on the Limits of Art and Poetry*), distinguished between the arts
of space and the arts of time. In the arts of space he included
painting and sculpture, which describe bodies in a given moment
of their existence and are quickly perceived by the viewer. The arts
of time, namely, poetry—in which fiction and music may be
included—take longer to be perceived.[1] Moreover, they do not
represent the most suggestive moment, as Lessing put it, which is
to say, "a single moment in the course of an action . . . the one
which is most suggestive and which serves most clearly to explain
what has preceded and what follows" (1895:91). Rather, they represent ongoing processes expressed by means of language, which is
also perceived in the course of time. Lessing wrote:

> That which the eye takes in at a glance, he [the poet] enu-
> merates slowly and by degrees; and it often happens that,
> by the time he describes the last trait we have already

forgotten the first. . . . To the eye the parts, once seen, are constantly present; it can scan them again and again. To the ear, on the other hand, those parts which have already been described are lost, unless the memory retains them. (1895:98)

For Lessing, elements and conventions of time operate more effectively in those arts in which the presentation in time is progressive, as in poetry, literature, and music. These definitions were later refined further and adapted to contemporary art, in which Lessing's distinctions are no longer so clearcut, but his basic principle remains valid.[2]

It is not surprising, then, that Shimeon Bar-Efrat opens the fifth chapter of his book on the poetics of biblical narrative with the following statement: "A narrative cannot exist without time, to which it has twofold relationship: it unfolds within time, and time passes within it. The narrative needs the time which is outside it in order to unravel itself by stages before the reader. . . . The narrative also requires internal time, because the characters and the incidents exist within time" (1989:141). In other words, it takes time to read a story—we cannot simply look at the text and take it all in, or even most of it. It is in the nature of language that we put one word after the other, and one sentence after another. This process takes time, which is called the "time of narration," meaning the time it takes to tell the story. This is external time, which is more or less known and shared by all readers. It may be a three-page story that takes a few minutes to read or a much larger book, which may last hours.

The other aspect of time is the internal one of the story, usually called "narrated time," which is the time described in the story itself. The author decides how to use this kind of time by choosing which period in the heroes' lives to depict, where to expand or shorten time, and what comes after what—all according to the author's purpose and rhetoric. As Bar-Efrat puts it: "The shaping of time within the narrative is functional and not random or arbitrary but, making a genuine contribution, in coordination and cooperation with the other elements, to the character, meaning and values of the entire narrative" (1989:142). Thus, the author is concerned with the element of time throughout the writing, while for readers the perception of this time is essential to the understanding of the story.

Time of Narration and Narrated Time

The time of narration of a biblical story is very short. How long does it take to read or to listen to a story that spreads over twenty to thirty verses? I may add that even a long story like that of Joseph is actually a string of short ones linked together by cause and effect: the story of the sale of Joseph (Genesis 37), Joseph and Potiphar's wife (Genesis 39), the dreams of the cupbearer and baker (Genesis 40), and all the rest. This obliges the author to manipulate the narrated time with great skill, because a brief story may cover a period of many years. For example, the story of Judah and Tamar (Genesis 38), which takes thirty verses, actually covers several decades, from Judah's marriage to the daughter of Shua to the birth of his sons—who could have been his grandsons—Perez and Zerah, to his former daughter-in-law, Tamar. Here the author had to juggle the time of narration and the narrated time by deciding how much time of narration to devote to the circumstances that left Tamar desolate, how much to devote to the encounter between Judah and Tamar, which left her pregnant, how much to Judah's recognition that Tamar had been more in the right than he, and so forth.

Such decisions involving the passage of time in the story and in its telling are especially difficult in biblical stories, which are not only very brief but also often part of one historical sequence that extends over thousands of years—from the creation to the fall of the First Temple (Genesis to Kings). Anyone who sets out to tackle such a long period, a matter of thousands of years, must be very conscious of the need to pass over some periods, or reduce them to a minimum time of narration, and must develop a technique of compression: how to cover in a short time of narration a very long period in the narrated time.

The study of biblical literature reveals a number of techniques of compression, including using lists, standard phrases, and summarizing statements to signal the passage of time.

Lists

In the opening of the Book of Judges the author evidently wanted to shorten the story of the conquest and settlement (Judges 1). To do this, the author lists the possession and dispossession of lands, following an order of tribes and territories. He starts with a report on the conquests of the tribe of Judah, which then serves as the basis for comparison with the conquests of the northern tribes, proceeding from south to north, from Benjamin to Dan.[3] The author of the Book of Chronicles, who found the system of listing in his sources, used it to compress all human history, from Adam to the death of Saul, into nine chapters, and to start his story with the transfer of the kingship from Saul to David (1 Chronicles 10).

Standard Phrases

The author who began the Book of Exodus wanted to inform readers that several generations had passed between the death of Joseph and his contemporaries (Exod 1:6) and the rise of the new Egyptian king who did not know Joseph (v. 8). To do this, he devised verse 7 as a string of verbs that imply that many years, decades, or even centuries, have passed: "But the Israelites were fertile and prolific; they multiplied and increased very greatly, so that the land was filled with them."[4] Similarly, the phrase "when Moses had grown up" (Exod 2:11) covers the entire period between Pharaoh's daughter finding the basket and the adult Moses going out to his kinsfolk. There are also examples of vague references to time such as "Some time afterwards" (Gen 22:1), which leave the reader to imagine how much time has elapsed.

Summarizing Statements

Using summarizing statements may also define the length of time passage. The conclusion of the story of Ehud son of Gera is one such example: "and the land was tranquil for eighty years" (Judg 3:30b).[5]

The use of chronological markers not only tells the reader how much time has elapsed, it may also serve more complex requirements. For example, in the story of the succession (2 Samuel 9–20 and 1 Kings 1–2), we are told that Absalom killed Amnon two years after the rape of Tamar (2 Sam 13:23). Then, "Absalom, who had fled to Geshur, remained there three years" (2 Sam 13:38). Having received his father's permission, he returned to Jerusalem, then "Absalom lived in Jerusalem two years without appearing before the king" (14:28). Then Absalom sent Joab with a message to his father, saying, "Why did I leave Geshur? I would be better off if I were still there. Now let me appear before the king; and if I am guilty of anything, let him put me to death!" (14:32), after which the king consents to see him. Together, these chronological markers tell us that seven years had passed since the rape, during five of which Absalom never saw his father, and in the meantime he "had three sons and a daughter whose name was Tamar" (14:27). These markers make it plain that the relationship between Absalom and David was extremely difficult, and they establish the source of Absalom's bitterness and harsh criticism of his father.[6]

I would add that every time there is a multitude or concentration of chronological markers, it is meant to draw the reader's attention to the tendency of the text and its emphases. Thus, for example, in the story of the rape of the concubine in Gibeah, there is a multitude of time markers: "They raped her and abused her all night long *until morning;* and they let her go *when dawn broke. Toward morning* the woman came back; and as *it was growing light,* she collapsed at the entrance of the man's house where her husband was. When her husband arose *in the morning . . .* and set out for home" (Judg 19:25-27, italics added). The reader is made aware of how long she lay at the entrance of the house, before the locked doors, with no one hearing her. Were the people inside sleeping all that time? In any event, only in the morning, when her husband wants to proceed on his journey, does he come across her, as a corpse. Here the markers can hardly be unintentional; they serve to emphasize the horror and the prolonged abuse by the people of Gibeah, suggesting the evil character of these people, one of whom was Saul. [7]

In contrast to the technique of compressing time, a common biblical device of highlighting especially important events is to extend time. The more important the subject matter, the longer its time of narration. We have seen how, when the author wished to incriminate Amnon, a fairly long time was devoted to the rape scene. As a rule, the reader should look closely at what scene in the story is the longest, which one enjoys a relatively long time of narration, and the means by which this is achieved. Repetition and the use of dialogue are two ways of extending narration that we will discuss.

Repetition

Repetition is the most notable method of extending the telling of the story. The author repeats a statement in the same words, or in other words, and thus extends the time of narration. The construction of the Tabernacle was an especially important subject in the world of the biblical authors, particularly the priests among them. Therefore, the discussion of the divine command and the execution of the Tabernacle is detailed and repetitive. The section of Exodus in which God gives Moses the command to build a Tabernacle, complete with detailed specifications for the structure and its contents, spreads over seven chapters (25–31). The detailed execution of this command fills six more chapters (35–40).[8]

Likewise, the story of Isaac's marriage to a non-Canaanite woman was of great significance to the author of Genesis 24, who, using repetition, spreads it over sixty-seven verses. First, the author reports what took place in Abraham's house, and how the patriarch described the mission and made his servant swear an oath to carry it out (vv. 2-9). Then the servant reaches his destination and prepares a series of signs there which, if they occur, would presage the success of his mission (vv. 10-14). Then a cycle of rehearsals begins: the first is when Rebekah appears and acts according to the awaited signs (vv. 15-21); and the second is made up of three: when the servant reaches the house of Bethuel and there relates what happened at Abraham's house (vv. 34-41), and his expectations (vv. 42-44), as well as the encounter with Rebekah (vv. 45-48), all of which lead Laban and Bethuel to conclude that "the matter was decreed by the LORD" (v. 50).[9]

Dialogue

Dialogue is another method of extending a story. A dialogue creates the closest match between the time of narration and the narrated time, as in a play. We have seen how this technique was employed in the story of Abraham's purchase of the Cave of Machpelah, which occurs entirely in the form of dialogue (pp. 51–53 above). Moreover, the matter of the purchase of the cave is mentioned repeatedly throughout the Book of Genesis (p. 53 above). The use of both techniques, repetition and dialogue, provides a key to the significance of the subject.

At times the use of techniques that extend the time of narration appears with the narrator's emphasis that the narrated time was actually short and even closely packed with events. This kind of contrast is especially the case with stories of miracles. For example, one gets the impression that the ten plagues of Egypt lasted days or even months, but not years. Throughout its fairly long time of narration (Exod 7—12:36), there are certain time markers, such as "the next day" (8:6; 9:6), and "early in the morning" (8:16; 9:13), "tomorrow" (8:19; 9:5), "this time tomorrow" (9:18), and the like, but not "after some months," or "after a year." This creates the impression of a short period of time. The biblical author knows that the effect of miracles is also heightened by their following one another in close succession. A single plague could be dismissed as a natural event that recurs from time to time and could be coincidental, but ten plagues one after another in a short period of time point to divine intervention. Therefore, when the biblical author wants to emphasize the effectiveness of miracles, he compresses a number of them into a short narrated time and extends their time of narration.

The Sequence of Time

Another feature that belongs in this discussion is the sequence of time. Time's natural movement is from past to present to future—the familiar chronological sequence. Modern literature favors deviations from this sequence. One genre that often does this is detective fiction. Such a story may open with the final event, perhaps a murder, with the story dealing largely with the events and circumstances that led up to it, thus uncovering the solution to the mystery. The psychological novel, too, often harks back to the hero's past. The biblical story, which claims to be a historical narrative, is naturally bound to the chronological sequence, yet nevertheless, it contains some deviations from it, and they are always significant and functional.

Analepsis

Sometimes the biblical author postpones an early detail, and the past event is mentioned late in the story. "An analepsis is a narration of the story-event at a point in the text after later events have been told. The narration returns, as it were, to a past point in the story" (Rimmon-Kenan 1983:46). For example, quite late in the story of Joseph (Genesis 37–50), when he torments his brothers by jailing them for three days and proposing that one of them remain behind until they bring their youngest brother, the brothers talk among themselves, saying: "'Alas, we are being punished on account of our brother, because we looked on at his anguish, yet paid no heed as he pleaded with us. That is why this distress has come upon us'" (42:21). But in the story of the sale of Joseph (chap. 37) there was no mention of his pleading with them. The author chooses to bring it up here, where it heightens the psychological state of the brothers with the weight of their guilt after all those years.[10]

Such a postponement is clearly functional because it helps the author to stress a particular situation or idea. The description of the reign of Solomon in the Book of Kings (1 Kings 3–11) is an example of how this method is used to highlight an idea. After describing Solomon's wisdom and his many achievements, the author passes to his later years and refers to his sins, including that he worshiped alien gods under the influence of his many foreign wives (1 Kings 11:1-13). Then the author describes Solomon's punishment and how the Lord "raised up an adversary against Solomon, the Edomite Hadad" (11:14-22), followed by Rezon son of Eliada (vv. 23-25), and finally Jeroboam son of Nebat (vv. 26-40). A close reading reveals that these punishments had threatened Solomon long before he was old, but the author, wishing to illustrate the principle of retribution and the connection between sin and punishment, mentions them only after he has described Solomon's sin. This is clearly a theological sequence rather than a realistic or mimetic depiction of events.

Prolepsis

"[A] prolepsis is a narration of a story-event at a point before earlier events have been mentioned. The narration, as it were, takes an excursion into the future of the story" (Rimmon-Kenan 1983:46). Prolepsis is quite characteristic of biblical stories. Shlomith Rimmon-Kenan has pointed out that "[P]rolepses [i.e., anticipations, or forward looks at events] are much less frequent than analepses [deferral, postponement, or flashback], at least in western tradition. When they occur, they replace the kind of suspense deriving from the question 'what will happen next?' by another kind of suspense, revolving around the question 'how is it going to happen?'"[11]

And it is precisely prolepsis that bears the tension of "what will happen next," which is common in biblical stories. This occurs because prolepsis supports an ideological principle: stating in advance what is going to happen illustrates God's control over history. God is depicted as knowing the news before it happens: "See, the things once predicted have come,/And now I foretell new things,/Announce to you ere they sprout up" (Isa 42:9; also 40:21; 41:4, 23; and elsewhere). Biblical literature applies this device in many different ways.

1. God or his angels reveal themselves and foretell the future. This motif appears many times, from the stories of the patriarchs in the Book of Genesis through the Book of Judges. Through divine revelation, Abraham receives the announcement of the birth of Isaac, the patriarchs receive the promise of the Land and of future descendants, and leaders like Moses and Joshua receive divine support. These passages in biblical historiography, describing the childhood of the nation, contain many such revelations of God or the angels.

2. Anticipation by means of dreams. Dreams in biblical stories are never meaningless. In the story of Joseph, for example, Joseph himself dreams twice (Gen 37:5-11), the cupbearer and baker dreams (chap. 40), and Pharaoh has two famous dreams, about the cows and the ears of grain (41:1-45). These dreams refer to the future and are a form of divine communication, which is why Joseph says, "Surely God can interpret [dreams]" (40:8). And Pharaoh describes the interpreter of dreams as "a man in whom is the spirit of God" (41:38).

3. Consulting God or other powers, such as "familiar spirits" or other magical powers is a means of learning the future. This method is revealing about the world of the authors and their audience alike, who clearly believed in this possibility of knowing the future (see Judg 1:1-2; 1 Sam 28:3-25).

4. The narrator reveals what will happen later. The narrator reveals the future, while emphasizing, of course, that this will happen because God wills it: "The LORD had decreed that Ahithophel's sound advice be nullified, in order that the LORD might bring ruin upon Absalom" (2 Sam 17:14b). Sometimes the author throws in a hint about the future. For example, the story of the sin of David and Bathsheba concludes with the words, "But the LORD was displeased with what David had done" (2 Sam 11:27b), a statement that clearly bodes ill for David. Sometimes the narrator puts in implicit anticipatory information and thus hints at the future—as in the case of Nahor's genealogy (Gen 22:20-24), which mentions Laban and Rebekah.[12] The reader will notice this only later.

5. The appearance of prophets. The most obvious form of foretelling the future is the appearance of prophets or seers. Biblical historiography has sometimes been described as prophetic, a label based on the central place of prophets in biblical historiography (see Rofé 1988a:75–105). In the Book of Kings, the appearance of prophets and the definition of history as the fulfillment of

prophecy (Von Rad 1956:74–91) are not only theological principles but artistic and editorial ones. The book progresses along a
path of fulfilled prophecies, with the editor stressing from time to
time that events did indeed unfold as the prophet had predicted.
These various means of anticipating events serve the biblical
theme that God directs and controls history. Reality is not accidental. Some is making things happen and directs them.

All the above examples served the same purpose: to show that
the use of time in biblical stories is calculated and deliberate. The
control that the omniscient and omnipotent God has over the
world is above all manifested in the control of time. It is no accident that the story of creation (Gen 1-2:4a) includes the fixing of
the seven-day, or sabbatical, week.[13] The management of time is
not merely a matter of the correlation or lack of correlation
between the time of narration and the narrated time, it is a central
value in biblical literature as a whole.

Nine

Place, Story, and History

Since the characters in the story-world exist, as we do, in space as well as in time, let us now look at the spatial aspect of the biblical stories.[1] Though space complements time, it has not received the same amount of attention in literary studies in general and the study of biblical literature in particular.[2] It is often said that the subject of time makes for a more sophisticated analysis, because it can be discussed in terms of the relationship between time of narration and narrated time, whereas a discussion of space has no equivalent concepts. We can examine the space of the story-world, but we rarely do it with the space of the text, because the space of the text is also measured in terms of time. The text is described as long or short in terms of how long it takes to read, not the physical size of the page, the letters, or the distance between the lines, and so on. As a result, the use of spatial concepts in literature has attracted little attention, compared with the use of time.[3]

If this is the case with literature as a whole, it is doubly the case with the biblical story. Hermann Gunkel's view that the aspect of setting is secondary and marginal has been widely accepted:

Very many legends are equally sparse in the description of
the accompanying circumstances. . . . In fact, the ancients
obviously knew nothing of intimate sentiments for the
land. We see no trace of feeling for nature in Genesis. The
fact that the Paradise narrative takes place under green
trees, the Hagar legends in the barren wastes of the desert,
and the Joseph narrative in the land of the Nile influences
the course of the account in individual details, to be sure.
The people clothe themselves with leaves; one loses one's
way in the desert and there is no water there. But it does
not determine the mood of the action in any way. (Gunkel
1997:xxxviii)

Gunkel regarded the plot and its unfolding as the core of
the biblical story and maintained that the description of a
location, which is static and might slow the pace of the story
and the progress of the plot, was left out of most biblical stories. This view was adopted by Shimeon Bar-Efrat, who devoted only a few pages to the issue of space in his book, *Narrative
Art in the Bible*.[4] As he puts it: "The biblical narrative is wholly
devoted to creating a sense of time which flows continually and
rapidly, and this is inevitably achieved at the expense of the
shaping of space. Because space is fundamentally static and
unchanging it is an alien element in biblical narrative, based as
it is primarily on presenting developments, which are a function
of time" (1989:196). By way of illustration, Bar-Efrat refers to
the construction of the Tabernacle as described in the Book of
Exodus: "Accordingly, the Bible does not provide us with a
description of the sanctuary which served the people of Israel in
the wilderness, or of the Temple which Solomon built. We do
have a very detailed account of the making of the sanctuary
(Exodus 35–40) . . . because in this way the flow of narrated time
is not hampered and the narrative continues its progress unin-
terruptedly" (1989:196).

This argument nearly ignores the fact that the passage about the Tabernacle appears in a construction of repetition: first in a highly detailed command, which extends over seven chapters, followed by a highly detailed description of the execution of that command, spread over another six chapters (a total of thirteen chapters, constituting a third of the Book of Exodus, and consuming considerable time of narration; see pp. 108–9). Needless to say, the repetition could have been avoided, for example, by using the formula "and it was so" after the detailed command instead of describing its execution. This is how the author deals with the story of the flood (Gen 6:5—9:17). After God gave detailed commands about how to build the ark and whom to take into it, the narrator merely reports that the command was carried out: "Noah did so; just as God commanded him, so he did" (6:22).

The detailed command to build the Tabernacle and the equally detailed description of its execution are meant to convey the centrality of this abode of God, due to its place in the author's beliefs and ideas. This was the reason for such a detailed description, which is driven by the verb "to make": "They made. . . . He made. . . ." The focus is on what they made, rather than how they made it, and the reader gets an itemized picture of the Tabernacle: its size, structure, internal arrangement, its vessels, dominant colors, and so forth. In other words, this is a detailed, even a double description of the sanctuary, which was a mobile construction in the space of the desert (see Brinkman 1992; Hurowitz 1992).

The biblical authors do not avoid describing large objects in space when they seem important enough. That is why, when we look at the depictions of spatial objects, we must consider the functional aspect—namely, when and why the authors lingered over this aspect and what use they made of it—as well as their minimalist technique. In any event, we should not expect the elaborate descriptions prevalent in modern fiction.

Some Functions of Place Indications

It rarely happens in the Bible that a location is left unspecified.
This happens in parables, which are presumed to be fictional. Parables are usually detached from space and time, so as not to be confined by the concrete and to appear part of a universal situation.
For example, when Nathan appears before David to reproach him
for the affair of Uriah and Bathsheba (2 Samuel 11-12), he tells him
a parable that opens with the words, "There were two men in the
same city, one rich and one poor" (12:1). The city remains name-
less, unspecified, in obvious contrast to the usual practice in biblical stories, which take pains to pinpoint the settings of events.
Naming the locations makes the story seem real, while leaving
them unnamed heightens the fictional quality of the narrative.

A biblical author who wishes to emphasize the historical nature
of the narrative will not fail to offer a geographic image with
topographic indications. For example, in the story about the
abduction of the girls of Shiloh (Judg 21:16-22), the author makes
sure of the identity of the town in question by referring to it as
follows: "The annual feast of the Lord is now being held at Shiloh.
It lies north of Bethel, east of the highway that runs from Bethel
to Shechem, and south of Lebonah" (21:19). Similarly, the reference to Ai is backed up by naming its neighbors: "Joshua sent
men from Jericho to Ai, which lies close to Beth-aven—east of
Bethel . . ." (Josh 7:2). And in the story of Gideon's chase after the
Midianites across the Jordan (Judg 8:4-21), the author takes pains
to provide landmarks: "Gideon marched up the road of the tent
dwellers, up to east of Nobah and Jogbehah . . ." (8:11). It is not
surprising that we cannot identify these locations, given that
thousands of years have passed since the events described. Moreover, it is possible that even many of the contemporary readers did
not recognize all the place-names. Nevertheless, unfamiliarity
with the named places does not detract from the historical feel
that they give to the narrative, and this feel of authenticity and
reliability was the sought-after effect.

The use of place-names is therefore a regular feature with a specific function: to serve the biblical authors' historiographical needs. This regular situation enabled the authors to apply this device to some unexpected purposes. Here are some examples.

1. Creating a historical character by means of geographic markers. Place-names give the story a realistic tone but do not provide sufficient information for a reconstruction of the scenes depicted. We may assume that if the author had meant to provide a historical record, he would have been meticulous in these references of places and would have provided the necessary spatial and topographical data for the purpose of reconstruction. However, we shall see that this was not the case in the two following examples.

The story about Ehud son of Gera (Judg 3:12-30), who killed Eglon king of Moab, is well-stocked with topographical markers, with the result that most commentators treat it as a historical event.[5] Some even tried to reconstruct it by following the named landmarks. Oddly enough, they obtained widely divergent results. According to Josephus, Eglon's palace was in the City of Palms, Jericho, meaning that the entire drama took place west of the Jordan, between the fords of the Jordan and Mount Ephraim.[6] But, according to Moshe Garsiel, the place where Eglon received the tribute was in some city far beyond the Jordan, possibly Kir Moab, Dibon, or some other important Moabite city (1977: 58–67). Thus, in his view, the events described took place between Mount Ephraim and some remote region in Transjordan. Making no attempt to choose between the diverse possibilities proposed by the commentators, who are supported by the same data, I do find it significant that such very different options can exist side by side (see Amit 1999a:171–98). The fact that the author avoided naming the key location—i.e., where Eglon received the tribute—makes for ambiguity, which is not dispelled by the statement that the City of Palms was conquered by Eglon from the Israelites, and that this could have been the popular name of any city known for its palms, not necessarily Jericho.[7] This vagueness enables Josephus and Garsiel to propose such very different geographical settings for the events. It clearly shows that the biblical author's use of topographical elements is not intended for systematic documentation or for future reconstructions. Now and then the author names places for decorative purposes, as a kind of poetic ornament that is not essential, which helps to create a historical atmosphere and a realistic depiction of events. The mention of "Pesilim, near Gilgal" (Judg 3:19, 26) and "Seirah" (v. 26) as landmarks where Ehud passed contributes to the atmosphere of genuine history, even though commentators have never been able to locate these places (see Soggin 1981:51–52).

Nor can Sisera's escape route be reconstructed (Judg 4): did he pass by Kedesh Issachar, or was it Kedesh Naphtali in the Upper Galilee? Does Kedesh in the southeastern part of Naphtali's territory (near today's Poriah) seem more likely (vv. 6, 9, 11)? Did Jael pitch her tent near the stream of Kishon in the west? Or near a tributary of the Kishon river, which crossed southeast of the Valley of Jezreel (vv. 7, 13), not far from Taanach and Megiddo, the one mentioned in Deborah's song as "Megiddo's water" (5:19-21)?[8]

These texts suggest that the author intended to create an impression of historical writing rather than an actual historical record.

2. The vague geographic reference as a hint that the story is fictional. The same method of using place-names can be applied to achieve the reverse—to blur the geographic location as a hint about the fictional nature of the story. We find this feature in the story of Job (1–2 and 42:7-11). Already the Sages noted that the story of Job was fictional: "Job never did exist, but as a parable" (*b. Baba Bathra* 15a). Though the Sages said this in order to resolve the difficult theological problems presented by the story, an examination of its spatial aspect supports their argument and shows that the authors used references of various and far places to hint that the story was a parable. We are told that Job lived in the Land of Uz (Job 1:1), which could be Edom (Gen 36:28; Lam 4:21), or Aram

(Gen 10:23; 22:21),[9] and the friends who arrived to console him came from different and distant places (Job 2:11): Teman in the East (Gen 36:11) or Tema in the South (Isa 21:14), Shuah in the East or in the North (Gen 25:2) and the unknown Naamah.[10] Though no one has ever succeeded in locating these place-names in the same geographical region, their names create an image of far-flung lands, giving the story the quality of a legend. We may conclude that the Sages' perception of the story of Job as a parable rests on the data in the story that hint at its fictional quality.

In much the same way, the mention of the various rivers in the Garden of Eden creates an air of mystery around the location of the garden. It is described as being in the East, in the place where the river divides into four: the Pishon, Gihon, Euphrates, and Tigris. All attempts to pinpoint the place where the Tigris and Euphrates join the Pishon and Gihon have failed, and this could have been a hint that the story may be regarded as legendary or parabolic.[11] I say "hint" because it is never made explicit. The text employs known names, but geographically they do not add up, which creates ambiguity. This makes the text accessible to various audiences—to the sophisticated audience that catches the allusions and concentrates on the meaning of the story, regardless of whether and where it did or did not happen; and to the less sophisticated audience, which is readily convinced by stories that seem historical.

3. Place in the service of ideology. The use of the place aspect in the Book of Chronicles shows that it can also be used for ideological purposes, to depict a world that is concerned in keeping with the desired aim rather than with the possible and the real. Describing the campaign of Sennacherib (2 Chron 32:1-23), the author evidently does not care to show the full extent of it, since the triumph of the Assyrians is meant to illustrate that, thanks to Hezekiah's purifications and the Passover celebration (vv. 29-31), Sennacherib's attempt to seize Jerusalem would fail.[12] He therefore stresses that Sennacherib intended only to breach fortified cities

(32:1), and it remains unclear what exactly the Assyrians achieved, such as whether his massive armies reached Jerusalem or not (v. 9), and if they were beaten by the angel of God at Lachish or in Jerusalem (vv. 21-22). This topographical ambiguity, a deliberate deviation from the narrative in 2 Kings 18:13—20:21, bends the place aspect to ideological ends. With ideology as the supreme concern, it is possible for Hezekiah and his men to dig a water channel to bring water into the city in a matter of days, when in reality the project took years to complete: "but with us is the Lord our God, to help us and to fight our battles" (2 Chron 32:8).

4. Derivation of place-names and historical awareness. In many biblical stories a place is given special prominence by means of the derivation of its name. Bible research calls these etiological place-name stories, meaning that they are told to explain the origin of a name.[13] Highlighting a place-name with a story that concludes with its derivation gives added significance to the events described and enhances the historical importance of their location.

Jacob dreamed about a ladder that reached up to heaven with angels going up and down it and the Lord standing above. When Jacob awoke he said, "This is none other than the abode of God, and that is the gateway to heaven" (Gen 28:17), and in the morning he named the place, which had hitherto been known as Luz, Bethel ("House of God"). The key word in this story is "place." It opens with a triple repetition of it (italics added): "He came upon a certain *place* and stopped there for the night, for the sun had set. Taking one of the stones of that *place,* he put it under his head and lay down in that *place* (v. 11). When Jacob awoke, his first reaction was, "Surely the Lord is present in this *place,* and I did not know it!" (v. 16); deeply moved, he added, "How awesome is this *place!*" (v. 17). And the narrator concludes with the words, "He named that *place* [NJPS: "site"] Bethel, but previously the name of the city had been Luz" (v. 19). This story, like many others of this kind, was intended to sanctify the local shrine, but this device also enhances the reader's involvement with the story. Such stories offer explanations for surrounding phenomena—in this case, explaining why and when Bethel was given its familiar name. It implies that the space in which one lives with its various sites are linked to one's roots and connected with one's historical and national past. In this way, the stress laid on the site of an event through the derivation of its name serves to heighten the reader's historical awareness.

5. Place as the main subject. As a rule, place is so significant that entire stories revolve around particular places. The association with a particular place can represent a connection to a country, an ownership of the land and its holy sites. Thus, Abraham's purchase of a burial site in Hebron is mentioned four times in the Book of Genesis (Gen 23; 25:9-10; 49:29-32; 50:13). Jacob's purchase of a parcel of land near Shechem for a hundred kesitahs (Gen 33:19) is mentioned again after the conquest of the land and the settlement of the tribes: "The bones of Joseph, which the Israelites had brought up from Egypt, were buried at Shechem, in the piece of ground which Jacob had bought for a hundred kesitahs from the children of Hamor, Shechem's father, and which had become a heritage of the Josephites" (Josh 24:32). David bought the land for the temple of Jerusalem from Araunah the Jebusite (2 Sam 24:24), and Ahab's father, Omri, bought the land of Mount Samaria from its lord, Shemer (1 Kings 16:24). During the Babylonian siege of Jerusalem, the prophet Jeremiah purchased land in Anathoth to signify that "Houses, fields and vineyards shall again be purchased in this land" (Jer 32:15).

6. Typological routes. The fact that Abraham had built altars to the Lord near Shechem, Bethel, and Hebron gave these places ascendancy over others. They ceased to be casual and became linked to the tradition of the forefathers through the sanctity of associated locales. Therefore, the route followed by Abraham becomes a typological one, to be followed by his descendants. Then Jacob came and built altars in the same places, signifying not only the patriarchs' link with the land but also their hereditary connection with each other, and that of the Israelite nation to those same places.[14] Similarly, Abraham's migration to Egypt, the risks he ran there and his return laden with possessions, foreshadow the migration of the Israelites to Egypt and their return laden with possessions (Exod 12:35).[15] These two migrations foreshadow the later one of the Judeans to Babylon and their return "with silver vessels, with gold, with goods, with livestock, and with precious objects, besides what had been given as a freewill offering" (Ezra 1:6).[16] In this way, the move from the land to Egypt under duress and the return from there becomes a meaningful symbolic and typological nexus.

7. Place as an intentional background. The choice of a place is never random. It is no accident that the formative period of the Israelite nation took place in the desert, which became the setting for divine miracles: the daily ones, like the manna and the quail, and the singular ones, like the sources of water, victory in battles, and so on.[17] Moreover, one way of demonstrating God's might is to display it in a strange place. For example, God protects Abraham in Egypt (Gen 12:10-20) and in Gerar (Gen 20:1), and shows his power over Pharaoh and his magicians—that is to say, over their gods.[18] Particular places, such as bodies of water, can serve to demonstrate God's power.[19] The God who commands the water can turn the Red Sea into dry land for the people to cross. God's universal power can also be demonstrated by showing the hero trying to flee from God to the ends of the earth or the bottom of the sea—as did Jonah, who was commanded to go to Nineveh but attempted to flee to Tarshish, and found himself in the belly of the fish, bearing out the words of the prophet:

And if they conceal themselves from My sight
At the bottom of the sea,
There I will command
The serpent to bite them. (Amos 9:3)

8. Place as hero. The reference to place is so significant that it may even be the leading figure of the story. The characters in the story of the concubine in Gibeah (Judges 19–21) are all anonymous, thus highlighting the place-names, notably Gibeah itself, which lies not far from Jebus (Judg 19:11-12) and Ramah (v. 13). We do not know the names of the Levite, his concubine, or their host in Mount Ephraim, but we do know where the events took place.[20] We know that the Levite and his concubine were received very decently in Bethlehem, in utter contrast to the frightful reception in Gibeah. Knowing that David came from Bethlehem and Saul from Gibeah reveals how the latter became pejorative by association in the case of Saul of Gibeah, and the former positive by association in the case of David of Bethlehem. It implies that a person reflects his or her birthplace, so what can you expect of a king who was born in Gibeah?[21]

In summary, place serves the biblical author's needs. When the author seeks to illustrate the power of the deity who rules over the whole world, a remote setting is chosen. When the author wishes to give the stories an air of historical reality, familiar places are chosen as the setting. At times, the place-names hint at the ahistorical character of the story or act as a direct reflection of a hero. The author may use this device to create typological routes, or the derivation of place-names can heighten the historical awareness. Therefore, the place aspect is always functional, and understanding its function in the story leads to a deeper, more comprehensive understanding. The experienced reader will examine what has been mentioned, how it is mentioned, how many times, where, and to what purpose.

Ten

Inherent and Added Significance

So far we have discussed the various components of the story. Now let us see how these components come together to give the story meaning. To do this, we shall examine two stories that have already been discussed from other points of view: the story of Amnon and Tamar (2 Sam 13:1-22), and the story of Naboth the Jezreelite (1 Kings 21).

The Story of Amnon and Tamar

The last chapter in Shimeon Bar-Efrat's book, *Narrative Art in the Bible*, "contains an analysis of an entire narrative according to the various features discussed separately in the preceding chapters" (1989:239). The selected story is that of Amnon and Tamar, and its analysis concludes with the following statement, which also closes the book:

These features serve to invest the narrative of Amnon and
Tamar with significance extending beyond the limits of the
narrative itself and fitting its wider context. In the light of
these connections and the thematic parallel between this
narrative and that of Bathsheba and Uriah (which both deal
with unlawful intercourse), Amnon's abuse of Tamar is to be
interpreted as David's retribution for his behavior towards
Bathsheba. (1989:282)

This conclusion suggests that the thorough analysis of the story
as a unit in itself leads not to its specific meaning but to its significance in a broader context. Does this mean that the story of Amnon
and Tamar has no significance by itself? Can the significance of a
story be understood only in its larger context? In fact, in this particular case, where the context is the royal succession (2 Samuel 9–20
and 1 Kings 1–2), the proposed significance—that it is retribution
for the sin of David with Bathsheba—could fit any story associated
with David's family that comes after Nathan's prophecy (2 Sam
12:7-12). Admonishing David, Nathan says, "Therefore the sword
shall never depart from your house, because you spurned me by taking the wife of Uriah the Hittite and making her your wife. Thus
says the LORD, I will make a calamity rise against you from within
your own house . . ." (2 Sam 12:10-11). Thereafter, all the events concerning the succession, from the rape of Tamar through the murder
of Amnon by Absalom and Absalom's rebellion against his father,
to the struggle between Adonijah and Solomon and Solomon's
accession (from 2 Samuel 13 to 1 Kings 2), may all be interpreted as
punishment for David's sin with Bathsheba. Since Nathan
announces all this in advance, perhaps we can do without the analysis of this story, or the stories that come after it. If the meaning of
the story is known in advance, why bother to analyze it? We may
even ask, what is the purpose of analysis? Is it sufficient to discover
the literary techniques used by the author just so that we may
admire them? Or perhaps its function is to discover how the literary
techniques contribute to the building of the story significance?

The assumption that each story makes a contribution to the whole, and therefore has a significance of its own, helps us to study it by itself—at least in the first stage, though it is an artificial one—with minimal attention to its context. Indeed, the fact that biblical stories are always part of a large, comprehensive work should lead us to examine first each story on its own and only later to examine it in context. This way we avoid imposing the context significance upon the story and thereby losing its singular distinction. On one hand, every biblical story is, metaphorically speaking, a link in a chain, so that analyzing a demarcated story is like studying a detached link; on the other hand, since the detachment is not done arbitrarily or crudely, but as a careful extraction with due attention to surrounding connections, it makes sense to examine it carefully from all angles, and only then to restore it to its place and see how it ties in, what it contributes to the general setting, and vice versa. Bar-Efrat chose to forgo the significance of the story as the sum of its components, preferring to observe the links as inseparable parts of the entire chain and from the vantage point of the chain.

The Bible scholar Ariella Deem, examining the significance of the story of Amnon and Tamar, asked what kind of love it was that Amnon had for Tamar, or rather, what Amnon's motives were in raping her (1979). She endorses the Sages' argument that Amnon's love for Tamar was not disinterested but "depended on some [transitory] thing" (*m. Aboth* 5:16), and she interprets the "interest" as "the fact that Tamar was Absalom's sister." As she sees it, Amnon wanted to turn Tamar into a whore and thus Absalom into a whore's brother. Deem argues that such a stain on Absalom's pedigree would annul the chances of fulfilling David's brilliant political dream of forming an Israelite-Aramaean empire ruled by Absalom, his half-Aramaean son (2 Sam 3:3): "Underneath the tale of passion, the affair of Amnon and Tamar tells a different story: the annulment of David's dream of an eternal kingdom by the grace of God, whose dynasty would begin with a chosen heir, descendant of the patriarchs, the son of the king of Israel and an Aramaean mother—Absalom" (1979:107). The imperial dream that Deem describes stretches back as far as the genealogical horizon of the patriarchs. The story of Amnon and Tamar, which she regards as replete with typological symbols from the patriarchal tradition, represents a turning point in the history of the nation, disguised as a story of love and passion. She interprets the character of Amnon as that of a narrow-minded nationalist or an aggrieved son who fears that the kingship might be taken away from him and who chooses to defend his position by sexual means. Therefore, the true impulse in this story is neither love nor lust. As Deem puts it, the narrator is being "disingenuous" or untrustworthy, enticing his audience with "psychological motivation," when what he really has in mind are historical upheavals.

To my mind, interpreting this story as a tale of historical reversal is a kind of *Derash*—that is, homiletical exegesis, which some may define as sophisticated ideological reading. Not only does this interpretation conflict with the poetics of biblical narrative by presenting the narrator as untrustworthy, it also attributes to David an Aramaean ambition, based entirely on lacunae and gap-filling, rather than on textual data. It rests on a narrow notion of a union between Geshur and Israel, which has no foundation in either biblical or external sources. It is said that the exegete "introduces into the observed text intentions and notions of his own, consciously or sometimes unconsciously. In other words, the exegete's interpretation is subjective" (Melamed 1975:6). Deem's interpretation, which ascribes to the text ideas of her own without any solid evidence, is a subjective interpretation, whose causes and motives may be interesting in themselves but do not concern us here.

I am convinced that the attempt to elicit the explicit or implicit significance of a story by studying its various components, tying up as many of them as possible in a logical way, and paying close attention to its nuances and subtleties, can direct the interpreter to the plain interpretations, known as *Peshat*. When we examine the story of Amnon and Tamar by itself and consider all the devices used in it, the conclusion seems inescapable that its purpose is to lay a heavy charge against Amnon. The story is a document that condemns Amnon, while building up sympathy for Absalom.[1]

In previous chapters we discussed the various constituents of stories: openings and structures, the shaping of the plot, the narrator and the characters, and time and place, and we even touched upon method of presentation, namely, the style. By examining the story of Amnon and Tamar we shall see how all the elements combine to serve the central objective, which is to depict Amnon as a thoroughly bad character and thus build up sympathy for Absalom.

The story opens with Absalom, Tamar's brother, and concludes with him sharing Tamar's pain and nursing hatred for his half-brother. The two men are juxtaposed from the start, yet with a curious imbalance: Absalom is described briefly and Amnon at some length. The latter is the brother who is in love, but for some reason his love is focused on Tamar's virginity and on his desire "to do anything to her" (2 Sam 13:2).[2] This imbalance continues in the story's two climaxes: that of the plot (the change), in this case, the unusually long scene of the rape (vv. 8-18; these eleven verses take up half of the story), and the structural climax (the fourth scene in a three-and-four structure, pp. 64–65 above), in which Absalom takes Tamar under his protection, itself a short scene (two verses).

The scene of the rape also shows a marked disproportion in the time of narration: Amnon has three scenes to himself and Absalom only one brief scene (sixteen verses [3-18] against two [19-20]). It is reasonable to assume that such disproportion is tendentious, designed to put the emphasis on Amnon's bad character. Indeed, Amnon's image grows rapidly worse. If, to begin with, he is suspected of having vile intentions, it soon becomes evident that he has planned everything. The focus on the planning makes it impossible to regard the rape as a spontaneous act. In turns out that both the wise Jonadab and King David were duped by the cunning Amnon. The scene of the rape, which is the climax of the plot, reveals Amnon as both vicious and brutal. The phrase "he overpowered her" tells us that Tamar fought with Amnon. The author builds up the scene of the rape as a double climax: the first is the rape itself (v. 14), the second is Tamar's humiliating ejection from Amnon's house (vv. 15-18). For Tamar, the latter is even worse than the former; as she puts it: "Please don't commit this wrong; to send me away would be even worse than the first wrong you committed against me" (v. 16).

In terms of characterization, the technique of contrasts is most noticeable. The worse Amnon looks, the more positive Absalom appears. In the same way Tamar's words and conduct intensify the negative depiction of Amnon. The author shows Tamar's various attempts to prevent the rape. Her speech (vv. 12-13) combines the family aspect ("brother"), the human and personal ("Don't force me. . . . Where will I carry my shame?"), and the social-cultural ("Such things are not done in Israel! . . . You will be like any of the scoundrels in Israel!"). And if this were not enough, she concludes with a practical suggestion: "Please, speak to the king; he will not refuse me to you." By contrast, what the author has Amnon say after the rape makes him even more loathsome: "Get that woman out of my presence, and bar the door behind her" (v. 17). Amnon does not wish to see or hear Tamar's pleading; he cannot even refer to her by name. She embodies his shame, his being one of the scoundrels of Israel, unfit for kingship, and so she must be driven out.

In this story the marginal figures also play a role. Thus, for example, when Amnon wishes to eject Tamar, he calls his servant who appears at once, obeys his master's order, and bars the door after Tamar. This raises the question about why the servant did not come in when Tamar was struggling with Amnon? He was apparently nearby. This implies that Amnon had actually warned his servants not to intervene and to enter only when he summoned them. Also, there can be no doubt that the handling of the time element in this story is designed to disparage Amnon, which is why the rape scene is so long.

Spatially, this is a story of houses. David sends a message home to Tamar, telling her to go to Amnon's house. The author makes it clear that she had no reason to be fearful because there were other people in Amnon's house. Yet she is raped and then ejected and the door barred after her.[3] The scene ends with Absalom taking Tamar to his house: "And Tamar remained in her brother Absalom's house, forlorn" (v. 20).[4]

The story concludes with the narrator reporting both David's thoughts and Absalom's thoughts and commenting on them. He informs his readers that David loved Absalom because he was his firstborn, and that this was also the reason for not admonishing him (pp. 25–27 above); also, that Absalom hated Amnon, adding, "because he had violated his sister Tamar" (v. 22). And if the biblical narrator is always right, we have no reason to assume that Absalom's hatred stemmed from a desire to supplant Amnon as David's heir (pp. 128–29 above).

In sum, an examination of the story as an independent entity, and the observation of its various angles, reveals that it was designed to have a significance of its own—namely, to depict David's son, Amnon, as one of the scoundrels in Israel, unfit to reign, and by contrast, show Absalom as the better son, and so gain the audience's sympathy. According to this analysis, the story of Amnon and Tamar could serve as a reservoir of sympathy for Absalom.

The Story of Naboth's Vineyard

Another story, which has already been discussed and was also given a variety of interpretations, is that of Naboth's vineyard (1 Kings 21).[5] In order to deduce the meaning of the story, I have chosen to present two short interpretations that use literary criticism. The first argues that the main purpose of the story is to denounce marriage with foreign women,[6] while the second maintains that it is meant to illustrate the king's responsibility for whatever happened in his kingdom.[7] Which interpretation is consistent with most of the components of the story, and which is not? What should we expect from a story that is meant to lead to a particular conclusion?

We start with the first interpretation, which sets the boundaries of the story of Naboth's vineyard between verses 1 and 16.[8]

> What then is the message of the vineyard story? If we recapitulate our findings, saying that in the fifth or fourth century an author retold the old story of Naboth, shifting the guilt from King Ahab (2 Kings 9:25-6; 1 Kings 21:1-16), the aim of the present narrative becomes all too obvious. Jezebel, the sinner and seducer, is the foreign wife of Ahab. Through her, foreign women in general are stigmatized. The historical setting is the fight of Ezra and Nehemiah against intermarriage . . . it voices the complaint of the oppressed against the upper class, elsewhere vented by Nehemiah, Malachi and Trito-Isaiah as well as the protest against intermarriage as broached by Malachi, Ezra and Nehemiah. (Rofé 1988b:101–2)

If the story of Naboth's vineyard was designed to decry marriage with foreign women, we would have expected the foreign wife to figure at the start of the story, and moreover, that her depiction would stress her foreignness or at least suggest it. Yet when we examine this story by itself, we find that there is no reference or hint to her being foreign. In fact, the reader only knows about her being the daughter of King Ethbaal of Sidon from the earlier description of Ahab's reign in the Book of Kings (1 Kings 16:31). In this story, Jezebel is shown to be a domineering woman, willing to use any means in order to get what her husband wants.[9] Does she need to be a Sidonite to have such a character?

Moreover, if the story was meant as an attack on marriage with foreign women, surely this fact would have figured in God's denunciation against Ahab. Yet God sends Elijah to chastise Ahab for murdering and inheriting—not for his marriage to a foreign woman. Although, according to Rofé, this part of the story was written by another hand, it is strange that this hand ignored the main purpose of the story and did not use the opportunity to rebuke Ahab on this main issue, too.

And again, if that was the intention, why is there no reference in the plot to the worship of alien gods? There is not even one mention in this story of Jezebel's prophets of the Asherah, or the house of the Baal that Ahab had built in Samaria. Significantly, Yair Zakovitch and Alexander Rofé, the authors of the two interpretations mentioned above, agree that the third-person admonitory prophecy in this story (discussed on pp. 30–31 above) is a late insertion by the editors of the Book of Kings. When we ignore this insertion, not a single hint is left on the issue of idolatry—yet marriage to foreign women was opposed chiefly because they tended to draw their husbands to worshiping alien gods, as in the case of Solomon: "King Solomon loved many foreign women. . . . and his wives turned his heart away . . . after other gods, and he was not as wholeheartedly devoted to the LORD his God. . . . And he did the same for all his foreign wives who offered and sacrificed to their gods" (1 Kings 11:1-8). The absence of those expected elements suggest that this story could not have been meant to warn against foreign wives because of their alien religious influence, either explicitly or implicitly.

Rofé's other intention, relating to "the complaint of the oppressed against the upper class," would have fit the story's components much better if he had included Ahab among the upper class and not only Jezebel and the nobels, who were the "freemen" (*haḥōrim*).

The other interpretation—that the story was intended to emphasize the ruler's comprehensive responsibility—fits the story's components much better. Zakovitch puts it this way: "The Tale of the Vineyard, then, is not one of the Elijah stories, not a tale told to glorify the prophet and his deeds, but rather a moral lesson, in the style of other 'once there was a vineyard . . .' parables. Its object: to teach that a ruler is responsible for whatever is carried out in his name, irrespective of his efforts to remain ignorant" (1984: 398–99). The story opens and closes with the ruler. It opens with Ahab, king of Samaria, who owns a mansion in Jezreel, and ends with a humbled and contrite Ahab.

The plot unfolds in a linked progression that shows Ahab as the prime mover. If Naboth had not rejected Ahab's offer to buy his vineyard, then Ahab would not have gone to bed "dispirited and sullen" (1 Kings 21:4), and Jezebel would not have entered the picture, because she would not have written in his name to the elders of Jezreel, they would not have held a show trial, and Naboth would not have been stoned to death. The chain of events was set off by Ahab, who also tried to shirk his responsibility by having others obtain the vineyard for him. Had this not been the aim of the story, there would not have been emphasis on Jezebel's use of the king's name and his seal. It shows that, as far as the elders of Jezreel were concerned, the letters carried Ahab's authority, even though Jezebel had sent them and they reported to her that the order had been carried out. If this had not been the aim of the story, then in the scene of the admonition the author would not have confronted Ahab with the prophet, and the latter would not have delivered God's accusation of murder rather than of idolatry.

The use of the spatial dimension also supports this interpretation. Ahab meets Naboth in the vineyard in the first scene and hears God's devastating reproof in Naboth's vineyard in the fifth scene. This spatial symmetry suggests an instance of measure for measure: the site of the crime is also the site where the punishment is pronounced (see also pp. 55–56 above). This interpretation puts the stress on the ruler's responsibility for the events in his kingdom and corresponds better with the story's components.

Moreover, we should consider that a story may well stress several ideas or contain more than one meaning.[10] If so, then all meanings that fit most of the story's components are equally valid. And so it is in the story of Naboth's vineyard. We have rejected the interpretation that the story was part of the struggle against foreign marriages because it does not fit the story's components. But should someone argue that it concerns the status of monarchy in Israel, not merely the king's responsibility, the answer would be to test it against the story's components. And indeed such an argument may in fact stand up.[11]

It is also a reasonable assumption that the author did not arbitrarily choose to highlight the principle of the king's responsibility by means of a misappropriated vineyard. Clearly, the depiction of the king as a ruler who is far from being omnipotent and who must obey the divine commands and abide by social morality is inseparable from this story, as the examination of its components shows. The very opening of the story emphasizes the contrast between the king and his subject by juxtaposing palace versus vineyard. The conversation between Ahab and Naboth shows that the king is confident that everything can be obtained with money, or something of monetary value, to which his subject responds by speaking of his ancestral land and of God.

As the plot progresses, the mighty king appears to achieve his purpose: Naboth is murdered, and the king inherits the vineyard. But at this stage God intervenes, through his prophet, and informs the king that Naboth's blood would be avenged. A king who does not establish justice in his realm and who robs his subjects is an enemy of the prophet and, hence, of God. Ahab's exclamation at the sight of Elijah, "So you have found me, my enemy" (1 Kings 21:20), leads up to the recognition that he himself has become God's enemy, at which point he shows repentance and his punishment is deferred. In Israel, the king himself is a subject in God's service.

We see that this story, like others, can sustain and embody several meanings—while commentators can heap even farfetched interpretations upon it. The interpretation of the story of Naboth's vineyard as part of the struggle against foreign wives is not an inherent significance but an added one, an attempt to elicit something it does not contain. The Sages said that the Bible has seventy faces, or aspects, but that is not to say that they are all equally valid. Some faces illustrate what the story's interpreters wish to find in it, while others shed light on the integration of the story's components. The reader should be able to distinguish between interpretations that serve the needs of the interpreter and his/her readers and interpretations that strive to remain faithful to the significance that arises from the fashioning of the story.

Eleven

The Story and Its Context

WE HAVE LOOKED AT THE BIBLICAL STORY as a separate link in a chain. Let us now look at the chain as a whole, and how its individual links are incorporated in it. A discussion of the whole and its parts, and the place of the parts in the whole, is especially applicable to biblical stories, since they have come down to us as part of a larger entity, and since the demarcation of the individual parts, not having been done by an author or editor, is left up to the reader (see pp. 14–21 above). We shall also examine how the specific meanings we have discovered conform with the whole.

The Story of Amnon and Tamar

The story of Amnon and Tamar, which we have demarcated between verses 1 and 22 in 2 Samuel 13, is part of the larger story of David's sin and punishment, which is part of the Book of Samuel, which in turn is part of the Deuteronomistic history, which is part of biblical historiography.[1] For our purposes, the story of this particular link, the rape of Tamar by Amnon, can be examined in relation to the different circles that surround it.

In the previous chapter I proposed that the significance of this story, as a link in the series, is to expose Amnon, David's eldest son, as a scoundrel who is unfit to reign. I pointed out that the figure who is opposed to Amnon in this story, Absalom, is shown in a positive light. Let us now examine the wider context and see what this interpretation contributes to the comprehensive picture.

The depiction of Absalom as a positive figure affects the reader's impression of his later rebellion against his father. Reading about the rebellion in 2 Samuel 15, which describes Absalom's regal behavior "with a chariot, horses and fifty outrunners" (v. 1), his conduct at the city gates, with the narrator's harsh statement, "Thus Absalom won away [or *stole*, from the Hebrew *wayganneb*] the hearts of the men of Israel" (v. 6), one certainly gains the impression that he strove to succeed his father, even while David still lived. But reading about the relations between David and Absalom from the affair of the rape up to the rebellion, we perceive that David behaved unjustly and thoughtlessly, and we are moved by Absalom's disinterested love for Tamar and can even understand the causes of his bitterness about his father that grew in his heart during the seven years between the rape and the rebellion. While these factors do not justify Absalom's conduct, they certainly reveal different aspects of a character who is far from two-dimensional and oblige the reader to take note of the processes of his development and change. The fact that "the people supported Absalom in increasing numbers" (v. 12b) and that "[t]he loyalty of the men of Israel has veered toward Absalom" (v. 13) reveals that there was discontent with David's rule at various levels, and that there was more to Absalom's uprising than merely a rebellious son's lust for power.

In this light, I maintain that the story of the rape in the broader context is also intended to build up sympathy for Absalom, so that when we reach the story of the rebellion we would know that

Amnon was unfit to rule, that Absalom had good reason to criticize his father, and that King David was far from being a perfect man and a perfect king. This insight does not neutralize the argument that "Amnon's abuse of Tamar is to be interpreted as David's retribution for his behavior towards Bathsheba" (Bar-Efrat 1989:282; see p. 127 above). My argument is that the story also has a significance of its own, within its own boundaries, and that we gain depth and better understanding by seeing how this partial significance fits in with the wider context. There is another way that this viewpoint, recognizing David's weaknesses and his less-than-perfect justice, belongs in the circle of the Book of Samuel. Having described David's wars, the author summarizes the governmental structure of the kingdom and provides a list of the personages who held senior posts in it. The list opens with the statement: "David executed true justice among all his people" (2 Sam 8:15b). Another list of senior functionaries is given after the death of Sheba, son of Bichri, to confirm that David was once more ruler over all Israel (2 Sam 20:23-25). This time, however, there is no mention of David's justice. There is no doubt that in view of the preceding events—including the rape of Tamar and the struggle with Absalom—David could no longer be presented as dispensing perfect justice. In other words, the tragedy of Amnon and Tamar and the subsequent confrontation with Absalom were not only penalties and reward for David's sin with Bathsheba but also a means of illustrating a different aspect of David's personality. Evidently the revelation of David's darker and all-too-human face did not deter the deuteronomistic editor, who represents a wider circle, from depicting him as a model of a devout king (1 Kings 11:34; 15:3-5, 11; et al.). However, that darker face did not put off the Chronicler, who belongs in a still wider circle. The author of the Book of Chronicles saw fit to leave out most of the stories about David that appear in the Book of Samuel. By means of omissions, changes, and additions, this author managed to recreate a one-sided image of a just monarch who did only that which was right in God's eyes.[2]

The Story of Naboth's Vineyard

The story of Naboth's vineyard (1 Kings 21) is exceptional in its close context, namely, the cycle of Elijah stories (1 Kings 17— 2 Kings 2:18).[3] These stories are typically tales of miracles, or illustrations of the struggle against the worship of Baal, yet the story of Naboth's vineyard contains no miracles, and its central issue concerns socioeconomic justice. Biblical scholars generally maintain that this is a late story, a product of the influence of classical prophecy that raised the banner of social justice, and that the story drew its inspiration from a passage in the story of Jehu's revolt (2 Kings 9:25-26).[4] In other words, those who bring up this argument maintain that the Naboth story in 1 Kings 21 was interpolated at a late stage of the book's editing. We may therefore ask, to what extent does this story fit into its immediate context, the Elijah cycle, even though it does not concern Baal worship and was probably written by some late author?

I would say that the story of Naboth's vineyard meshes nicely. By interpolating this story in its present place, in the Elijah cycle, the editor achieved at least two objectives: first, Elijah was characterized as more complex, in line with the classical prophets, who chastised the kings not only for their worship of alien gods but mainly on social issues; second, Ahab was depicted in a very bad light as a manipulative king who shirked responsibility for his actions and who personified social injustice.

In addition to the immediate context of the Elijah cycle or the stories of Ahab's reign, we must not forget that these comprehensive stories form part of the still wider context of the Book of Kings. This brings us to another question: did the interpolation of this story, which deals with the king's responsibility and the expectation that he would dispense true justice, suit the editorial orientation of the Book of Kings? I believe that the answer must be yes. The subject of the Book of Kings is the history of the kingdoms of Judah and Israel, and the book addresses the question of who or what brought about the downfall of these two kingdoms.[5] The Book of Kings answers that the kings of Israel and Judah, who did not obey God and ignored the prophets sent by God to reprove them, caused the downfall of their kingdoms. Therefore, a story that emphasizes the king's responsibility and expands on the king's sins fits this context very well.

Moreover, the Book of Kings takes pains to note who was the first to commit sins in either kingdom, and whose sins were so great as to be unpardonable, and hence the decisive factor in God's decision to destroy the kingdoms. From this perspective, we see that the first king of Judah to commit fateful sins was Solomon, and in the case of Israel, Jeroboam son of Nebat. The king of Judah who was responsible for the divine decision to destroy the kingdom was Manasseh, and of Israel, Ahab, as stated in 2 Kings:

> Therefore the LORD spoke through His servants the prophets: "Because King Manasseh of Judah has done these abhorrent things—he has outdone in wickedness all that the Amorites did before his time. . . . assuredly, thus said the LORD, the God of Israel: I am going to bring such a disaster on Jerusalem and Judah that both ears of everyone who hears about it will tingle. I will apply to Jerusalem the measuring line of Samaria and the weights of the House of Ahab; I will wipe Jerusalem clean as one wipes a dish and turns it upside down." (21:10-13)

It is worth noting that here, too, the editor did not confine his indictment to the king's sins in cultic matters but added the following: "Moreover, Manasseh put so many innocent persons to death that he filled Jerusalem [with blood] from end to end—besides the sin he committed in causing Judah to do what was displeasing to the LORD" (2 Kings 21:16). Since the Deuteronomistic editors of the Book of Kings regarded Ahab as the greatest sinner in the Kingdom of Israel, he was a suitable leading figure in the story of Naboth's vineyard, in which he is accused, like Manasseh, of shedding innocent blood.

Reading the story of Naboth's vineyard in relation to the short passage in the story of Jehu's revolt (2 Kings 9:25-26) reveals several discrepancies. For example, in 2 Kings 9 it is stated that Ahab was guilty of the murder of both Naboth and his sons. There, it is a field rather than a vineyard, and it lies outside the city, rather than beside the king's palace; there is no mention of a show trial, only the murder of Naboth and his sons the previous night; nor is there any reference to Elijah. That is why, in spite of the discrepancies between the expanded story and the reference to the Naboth affair in the story of Jehu's revolt, the insertion of the former is quite consistent with its immediate context in the Book of Kings. Evidently these discrepancies did not bother the editor who inserted the story and regarded it as a meaningful contribution to the characters of Ahab and Elijah and to the ideas of the Book of Kings. The discrepancies are minor, but they help to shed light on the editorial methods and considerations.

The still wider context, that of biblical historiography in general, and even other biblical genres, such as the books of law and of prophecy, shows plainly that the king was expected to dispense true justice in his realm. At the same time, there is harsh criticism of the institution of monarchy, as shown by Samuel's warning regarding "the practice of the king" (1 Sam 8:11-17), the law of the king in Deuteronomy (Deut 17:14-20), and the prophecy of Jeremiah (Jer 22:1-9; 13-19; 23). Therefore, a story that accuses a king of social injustice fits these broader frameworks, too.

The Story of Judah and Tamar

Yair Zakovitch, in his article "'Go up, thou bald head; go up, thou bald head': Exegetical Circles in Biblical Narrative," compared the relationship between the individual story and its series of contexts to the circles formed by a stone dropped into water (1985:8). The wider they are, the weaker the stone's impact. This image may be clarified by the following example. The story of Judah and Tamar

(Genesis 38) is interpolated in the story of Joseph, just after the brothers sold him to the Ishmaelites and before he was bought by Potiphar, Pharaoh's chief steward. Most critical biblical scholars agree that the story of Judah and Tamar was inserted in this place by an editor.[6] This editor used the technique of "resumptive repetition," which, in this case, means that the opening words of the story of Joseph in Potiphar's household (Gen 39:1) echo the last words in the story of the sale of Joseph (Gen 37:36), and, picking up from there, return the reader to the point of departure by linking it to the original continuation.[7]

The commentators point out that the insertion interrupts the story of Joseph and does not accord with it chronologically, since if Judah married the Canaanite woman "about that time" (38:1)—namely, when Joseph was sold to the Ishmaelites—then the birth of Tamar's twins, Perez and Zerah, must have taken place in Egypt. Yet Perez's sons figure in the list, in Genesis 46, of those who went to Egypt (v. 12).[8] Already the Sages (*Gen Rab* 84:19) and, following them, some modern commentators noted the similarities between the inserted story and its immediate context in the story of the selling of Joseph (Genesis 37).[9] Just as the brothers showed Jacob Joseph's bloodied coat, saying: "Please examine it; is it your son's tunic or not?" (Gen 37:32), so Tamar says to Judah, "Examine these: whose seal and cord and staff are these?" (Gen 38:25). The author uses the same verb (root: *nkr*) in both questions and notes that the person questioned recognized the items, and in both cases there is an element of deception. Joseph's brothers deceive their father, and Tamar deceives Judah. Both stories feature a goat kid: in the story of Joseph, the brothers dipped Joseph's coat in kid's blood to make Jacob believe that a savage beast had devoured his son, and in the other story, Judah sent a goat kid by way of payment to Tamar. Some commentators interpret these parallels as a hint at divine retribution—specifically, that Judah's family tragedies are punishment for his role in the sale of Joseph (see n. 8).

But Frank Polak disagrees with this approach: "These tragedies took place long before Judah approached Tamar, so that the connection is, at most, circuitous. That is to say, these details do not add up, nor do they form a proper scheme of parallel and opposition" (1994:202). Nevertheless, he emphasizes that "since we cannot ignore these data, they may be viewed as mere allusions" (202). While some consider this interpolated story to fit neatly in its context, Polak argues that, despite the allusions, the connection is tenuous.

To choose between these two views, we need to clarify the purpose of the story of Judah and Tamar in itself. Without going into an extensive analysis, it strikes me that the author of this story meant to characterize the eponymous ancestor of the tribe of Judah and to depict the background of his link with his descendants, the House of David (38:28-30). We dealt with the character of Judah in chapter 6 and concluded that he is shown in a positive light—both by the author who took pains to explain Judah's motives and to illustrate his humanity and justice, and by God, who eventually rewarded him with male children, one of whom, Perez, would be the ancestor of David. This theme, dealing with the House of David and its place in the people's history, is not directly related to the story of Joseph. Moreover, the connection between Perez and David is not revealed in the Book of Genesis nor in the Book of Samuel, but in two late books: it is spelled out at the end of the Book of Ruth (4:18-22) and at the beginning of the Book of Chronicles (1 Chron 2:3-15).[10] The writer who described the circumstances of the birth of Perez (David's ancestor who is mentioned only in the Books of Ruth and Chronicles) and inserted it into the story of Joseph was an author/editor with a different objective in mind.[11] This author/editor was not concerned with the greatness of Joseph, the father of Ephraim and Manasseh, but with that of Judah. Therefore, it is a reasonable assumption that this is not an integral part of the story of Joseph and could have been left out without damaging the story of Joseph. On the contrary, without it, the story of Joseph would have gained fluency and continuity.

Why, then, did some editor nevertheless choose to interpolate this story in its present place, namely, between the sale of Joseph to the Ishmaelites and his purchase by Potiphar? The answer may be found both in the immediate context (the story of Joseph) and in the broader context (biblical historiography), and also in the recognition that biblical editing is not merely a cut-and-paste technique but a form of craftsmanship. By interpolating the story of Judah and Tamar in this place, the editor conferred on Judah a higher status than the rest of the brothers, except Joseph. This purpose fits neatly with the immediate context. The depiction of Judah as a positive character enhances his image in the story of Joseph, as a brother who shoulders responsibility and is thus superior to the eldest, Reuben. Judah is the one who proposes selling Joseph and thereby not only saves him from the brothers who want to kill him but also indirectly leads to his reaching Egypt (Gen 37:25-28). It is Judah, rather than Reuben, who persuades Jacob to send Benjamin to Egypt (Gen 42:37—43:15), and, finally, it is Judah who stands up to Joseph to urge him not to imprison Benjamin, and so causes Joseph to reveal himself (Gen 44:14—45:1). The combined story, presenting Judah in a favorable light, helps to draw attention to him as a salient figure from the start. By the time Judah acts as spokesman for his brothers in Joseph's court, the role seems natural. In other words, the favorable characterization of Judah accords well with his role in the story of Joseph.

Viewing this story in a wider context, in biblical historiography, the description of Judah in relation to Perez—an allusion to David—tilts the scales in Judah's favor. Despite Joseph's success in Egypt, which saved the family of Jacob for a time, we are reminded that it was thanks to Judah that Joseph was spared and reached Egypt. Therefore, in perspective, it is Judah who is worthy of the blessing:

> [Y]our brothers shall praise you,
> Your hand shall be on the nape of your foes,
> Your father's sons shall bow low to you. . . .
> The scepter shall not depart from Judah,
> Nor the ruler's staff from between his feet. . . . (Gen 49:8-12)

Judah, then, who represents not only the tribe of Judah but also the Judaean kingdom, is the lodestone of national aspirations. Placed where it is, the story has a special significance in the context of biblical historiography and provides a different view of the story of Joseph. The reader who catches the allusion to the link between Judah and David can see the achievements of Joseph, who represents Ephraim and the northern kingdom, in a different proportion, since, in the long run, the house of Joseph went into exile, and the hope of continued national existence lay with Judah, which remained the hope for a continuation of national life. On the other hand, one must know the Book of Ruth or the Book of Chronicles to understand the interpolated story in the wider context. In other words, the breadth of the context is contingent upon the reader's knowledge.

With regard to the editing method, the Sages and those who followed them were right to point out the visible ties connecting the interpolated story of Judah and Tamar to its surroundings (see p. 144 above). But Polak, too, is correct when he argues that "the connection is, at most, circuitous" (1994:202). The editorial technique mediates between the two arguments: the editors who decided to insert the story in this place did not patch it in crudely, but took pains to connect it to its immediate surroundings with fine ties, using repeated motifs and similar phrasing. That is why, though it is clearly a story that was imposed upon the text, it is neatly related to it. These are more than mere allusions, they are fine stitches that connect the insertion to its setting. However, once the story was set in its place, there was no avoiding the rise of interpretative circles around it. Thus, an examination of the story in its various contexts becomes a two-way process of enrichment: it enhances the framework, which in turn enhances and deepens the story itself.

Afterword

> For there is no end to literary study of a text, and the reader of
> the present work will surely feel that much else could, and
> indeed should, be said. . . . But then the analysis and survey
> given above make no claim to completeness; they are meant
> simply as a help to enable other readers to approach the text
> more nearly. (146)
> —Charles Conroy, *Absalom, Absalom!*

READING A BIBLICAL STORY and getting the most out of it is a
process that begins with demarcating the story's outlines, then
analyzing its text and its different aspects, from structure and plot
through characters and narrator, to time and place. And all the
while, observing the finest points of style is essential, since the
short stories we are examining employ minimalist and functional
means. The juncture where all or most of these aspects merge is
the story's significance—or significances, since there may be more
than one. Nor is that the end of it. It is then necessary to see how
the story fits into its graduated contexts. A context may be close,

such as a cycle of stories involving a particular individual, as the story of Naboth's vineyard is part of the stories of Elijah or Ahab. Or it may be wider, like the book in which the story and the cycle are embedded as in the case of the Naboth story and the Book of Kings. It may be a still wider context, such as biblical historiography or other relevant genres. We know that the subject of monarchy is also discussed in the books of law and of prophecy. Not every story is clearly an integral part of its context, like the story of Amnon and Tamar, which I described as a link in a chain because it belongs in the plot sequence. A story could have been inserted by some late editor, in which case the plot links may be marginal or nonexistent, and in their place are such phrases as "About that time . . ." or verbal and associative ties. In such cases, as with Judah and Tamar, it is necessary to see how the story was inserted in its place, and, more importantly, what it contributes to its surroundings, and how it is connected to the ever-widening circles of context, which have been compared to spreading circles in water.[1]

But what of the stone itself? Is it a piece of limestone that crumbles with time and the effects of wind and water? It seems to me, rather, that reading a biblical story is like observing a polished gem, and the more you examine it from various angles, the more you are captivated by the many facets of its brilliance.

Abbreviations

AB	Anchor Bible
AJSR	*Association of Jewish Studies Review*
AnBib	Analecta biblica
ASORMS	American Schools of Oriental Research Monograph Series
b.	Babylonian Talmud
BDB	F. Brown, S. R. Driver, and C. A. Briggs. *A Hebrew and English Lexicon of the Old Testament*
BEATAJ	Beiträge zur Erforschung des Alten Testaments und des antiken Judentum
BHK	*Biblia Hebraica*
Bib	*Biblica*
BibIntSer	Biblical Interpretation Series
BibSem	Biblical Seminar
BJS	Brown Judaic Studies
BLS	Bible and Literature Series
BM	*Beit Mikra*
EB	*Encyclopaedia Biblica*
FCB	Feminist Companion to the Bible
FOTL	Forms of the Old Testament Literature
GBS	Guides to Biblical Scholarship
Gen Rab	*Genesis Rabbah*
Gr.	Greek
Heb.	Hebrew

HSM	Harvard Semitic Monographs
HTR	*Harvard Theological Review*
ICC	International Critical Commentary
IDBSup	*Interpreter's Dictionary of the Bible: Supplementary Volume*
ISBL	Indiana Studies in Biblical Literature
ITL	International Theological Library
JANESCU	*The Journal of the Ancient Near Eastern Society of Columbia University*
JBL	*Journal of Biblical Literature*
JPS	Jewish Publication Society
JSOT	*Journal for the Study of the Old Testament*
JSOTSup	Journal for the Study of the Old Testament: Supplement Series
LCL	Loeb Classical Library
m.	Mishnah
MLBS	Mercer Library of Biblical Studies
MT	Masoretic Text
NJPS	*Tanakh: The Holy Scriptures: The New JPS Translation according to the Traditional Hebrew Text*
OBS	Oxford Bible Series
OBT	Overtures to Biblical Theology
OTL	Old Testament Library
Proof	*Prooftexts: A Journal of Jewish Literary History*
Ps-Philo	Pseudo-Philo
Radak	Rabbi David Kimhi
Rashi	Rabbi Solomon Isaac
SBL	Society of Biblical Literature
SBT	Studies in Biblical Theology
SemSt	Semeia Studies
SSN	Studia semitica neerlandica
TA	*Tel Aviv*
TTZ	*Trierer theologische Zeitschrift*
TUMSR	Trinity University Monograph Series in Religion
USQR	*Union Seminary Quarterly Review*
var.	variant
VT	*Vetus Testamentum*
VTSup	Supplements to Vetus Testamentum
ZAW	*Zeitschrift für die alttestamentliche Wissenschaft*

Notes

1. The Power of Stories

1. On the formative function of biblical stories, for example, of education and giving instructions and the combination of the "useful and the sweet," see Amit 1999a:10–14.

2. On the importance of stories see Ryken 1984:33 and Amit 1999b:11–14, 108-15.

3. There are scholars who assume that "most of the literature of the Old Testament had a long and often complicated oral prehistory" (Tucker 1971:6). This assumption, which is already expressed in Hermann Gunkel's commentary on the Book of Genesis (1997), was developed in Scandinavian research (Nielsen 1954) and was adopted to a greater or lesser extent by many others (for example, Culley 1963). More recently, Niditch (1996) has emphasized the continuity of the oral tradition and its interaction with literacy. This is accepted by nonbiblical scholars as well (for one example, see Yassif 1999:8–37).

4. As Culley put it: "The existence of an authoritative written text is insurance against change or error" (1963:117). Needless to say, in the process of transmission even written material can be changed, either because of copyists' errors or editorial intent.

5. One example from Long: "[O]ral literature is an ephemeral phenomenon which is actualized in the complex interaction of performer, audience, and occasion" (Long 1976:193).

6. Among others, see Long 1976:195; Cassuto 1972a:68–70; Culley 1976. Form-critical scholars have already described it (Habel 1965). Alter borrows the term "type-scene" from the scholarship of the Homeric epics (1981: 47–62). See also Niditch 1996:8-24.

7. See, for example, Muilenburg 1953; Alter 1981:88–113; Sternberg 1985:365–440.

8. Thackeray and Marcus (1977) note that in the interchange of "harlot" and "innkeeper," Josephus "follows the Palestinian interpretation found in the Targum on Josh 2:1, where the noun is translated *pundekita,* Gr. Πανδοκεύτρια or πανδόκισσα, 'innkeeper'" (*Ant.* 7.137).

9. The use of the root ἀρχειν (*archein*) with its nouns is common in Greek. The parallel Hebrew root *šlṭ* appears mostly in late Hebrew, see BDB 1020.

10. For a later dating, after Bar Kochba Revolt (135 C.E.) and before the eighth century C.E., see Zeron 1973:xviii, 45–51, 231–33.

11. Harrington reads here "Ashdod and notes Var. 'Gaza,' which is the reading of Judg 16:1. The Hebrew *'azata* (to Gaza) could have been mistranslated into Gr. as Azōton. But Ps-Philo frequently changes the places of biblical events" (1985:356).

12. I do not refer here to problems of textual criticism. The verb "learned," which appears in brackets (see the third version, which is taken from the NJPS translation, p. 5 above) is missing in the MT. Usually, scholars complete the text according to the Septuagint reading: "were told." See p. 25 below.

13. They used the similarity of the Hebrew roots *zny,* from which derives the noun *zona* (whore), and *zwn,* which is linked to *mazon* (provision). See Rashi in the wake of the Targum and Radak's criticism. This interpretation exists also in the Christian tradition, see Krouse (1949:74, n. 21), who also mentions John Marbecke's description from 1574 as an example.

14. On this story and its place in the whole cycle, see Exum 1976:159–64.

15. For an extensive discussion of these subjects, see Amit 1991a:282–85. On the verbs for the descent of the spirit on Samson, see Alter 1990.

2. Story Scholars and the Role of the Reader

1. Wellhausen 1957 [1885] and classical introductions to the Hebrew Bible, for example, Driver 1913a.

2. In the words of Weiss (1984:37 n. 24): "The mediaeval peshat ("literal") commentators often show an acute awareness of subtleties of style and meaning. But their hermeneutic includes a vigorous separation of form and content which, in the final analysis, precludes any real compatibility between their exegesis and modern close reading."

3. Awareness to literary issues can be found in the works of other commentators, as, for example, Skinner 1963.

4. In Buber 1994a:120n9), the editors explain: "A leitwort etymologically is a 'leadword,' a word that leads or guides the reader through the thickets of the text." See also Buber 1994a:114n1. For a discussion on Buber's definition and its multipurpose, see Amit 1989.

5. For the English translation, see Weiss 1984, especially the introduction (1–46), where he differentiates between the changing approaches to the understanding of the literary text and changing approaches in modern biblical scholarship (as well as a rich bibliography).

6. See also Weiss 1963b, 1965, and 1983.

7. See Auerbach 1957, Alonso-Schökel 1961, and a summing-up description in Robertson 1976.

8. See also Sternberg 1985:186–229.

9. See also Sternberg 1985:10–11, 516 n. 7, 524 n. 1.

10. On this dating in contrast to that of others, see Amit 1999b:20–33.

11. For a short but systematic survey of the past fifty years of this study, see Polak 1994:433–40. See also Rosenberg 1992. For criticism of being dissociated from issues of gender, see Bal 1991.

12. See, for example, Na'aman 1990:294, 343.

13. The division into chapters was introduced by Stephen Langton of Canterbury (ca. 1205).

14. Skinner 1963:39–41 argues that it concludes with verse 3 and that verse 4a "is in all probability a redactional insertion" (40).

15. The second half of verse 31, "He had led Israel for twenty years," concludes the whole cycle of Samson stories. For a discussion about these boundaries, see Amit 1999a:272–74, 282–89, 304–7.

16. See Perry and Sternberg 1970:631–42 in response to Arpali 1970: 587–89 and Simon 1970:598–600.

17. Arpali 1970:587–88 and Perry and Sternberg 1970:637.

18. On the different meaning of Judges 17–18 and 19–21 and of their appearance at the end of the Book of Judges and its meaning, see Amit 1999a:310–57.

19. Arpali 1970:588; Simon 1970:599–600.

20. The MT mentions only Elkanah but in the Septuagint the subject is Hannah.

21. According to Simon 1997:1–4, the story contains these parts: 1 Sam 1:1-28 plus 2:11a plus 18-21a. Indeed, in his new and revised publication of a former article (for details, see Simon 1997:xvii), he felt the need to change the title of the same outline, giving it a new title that stresses the motif of giving: "The Birth of Samuel: Miracle and Vow, Divine Gift and Maternal Consecration."

22. For another dynamic reader's role, gap-filling, which will not be discussed here, see Perry and Sternberg 1968 as well as Sternberg 1985: 186–229.

3. A Biblical Story alongside Biblical Criticism

1. See also Amit 1999a:1–24.

2. See also Alter 1999:70.

3. This is in the NJPS translation. The Septuagint (1879) reads: "and it was reported to the Gazites" (339).

4. See also Moore 1966:348–50; Soggin 1981:250–53; and many others.

5. I used italicized words ("not": in Hebrew, w^e*lo*) in order to show the place where the eye of the scribe/copyist jumped from the first occurrence to the second, gapping the intervening MT. Critical commentators agree that this is a case of homoioteleuton or haplography. For example, see Driver 1913b:301; Hertzberg 1972:322 n.b. This plus is also attested by Josephus, *Ant.* 7.173 (Thackeray and Marcus, trans. 1977) and lately by 4QSam^a from Qumran, see Ulrich 1978:84–85.

6. This analysis is generally accepted in critical commentaries; see Driver 1913b:20–21; Hertzberg 1972:26; and many others, including, more recently, Alter 1999:7.

7. See Moore 1966:233. For an analysis of Judg 8:27a and the clause 27b as an editorial deviation, see Amit 1999a:231–32, 260–62, as well as for the explanation for the term "editorial deviation" on 21–22.

8. For a detailed analysis, see Zakovitch 1984:399–401, especially n. 48, which stresses that "scholars dispute the precise extent of the Deuteronomic insertion." According to Gray 1977:435–36, the insertion contains vv. 20-29; see also Long 1984:224–25, who mentions "series of Dtr supplements in vv. 20b-29," and additional bibliography there. Uffenheimer 1999:374–75 minimizes the insertion to vv. 25-26. See also Rofé 1988b:94–95.

9. This is not the place to decide the scope of the insertion (see note 8 above) since this is an ongoing debate among commentators. The main point is that most of them are convinced that there is an editorial insertion.

10. Comparison of manuscripts enriched this kind of research, see lately Tov 1992:313–49.

11. See Driver 1913b:27–28; Hertzberg 1972:29; Simon 1997:30–33; and likewise many others. An interesting view is to be found in Weitzman 1997:113–17.

12. According to Simon, such a prayer-song does not fit the noble character of Hannah (1997:4, 30–33).

13. See Polzin 1989:30–36, especially n. 19 (p. 232). See also the broad dis-cussion of Weitzman (1997), who focuses on songs and stories.

14. There is no reason to assume that a late story cannot depict an early period. On the dating of the Book of Samuel, as written after the establishment of the monarchy, see Amit 1999b:20–33, 42–48. Many critical scholars adopt Noth's assumption (1981) and regard the book as part of the Deuteronomistic History. See, for example, McCarter 1983:14–17. Van Seters describes the Court History as a post-Deuteronomistic addition (1983:277–91).

15. Compare Hannah's Song to Psalm 113. There is a similarity to the interweaving of various psalms in the sequence of the Book of Chronicles. See 1 Chron 16:8-36; 2 Chron 6:41-42. See also Jonah 2:3-10; Exod 15:1b-18. For more examples, see Weitzman 1997.

4. Beginnings and Endings

1. On the exposition in literature generally, see Sternberg 1974 and 1978.

2. According to Rashi, "same language" is the holy language, and the Hebrew *devarim 'aḥadim* ("same words") means being of the same mind. On this opening and for three more interpretations that Rashi proffers, see Greenstein 1989:47–49.

3. The Masoretic Text has here a scribal error. It reads there that Samuel was buried in Ramah *and* in his own town. As it is not likely that he was buried twice, the Septuagint, the Vulgate, and several Masoretic manuscripts have only "in his town." Some scholars hold that this was an adhesion of words and should read "in his own town of Ramah," as in the NJPS transla-tion used here.

4. According to Simon (1997:73–74), the exposition includes v. 7, but see Bar-Efrat 1996a:344.

5. On the special role of the biblical exposition, see Amit 1999a:120–35.

6. On the ring structure of this story, see Simon 1997:74; and Bar-Efrat 1996a:344.

7. Indeed, the exposition ends in v. 5. On the two parts of this exposition, see Sternberg 1974:52–61; and 1978:23–29.

8. Gunkel 1997 has already noted that the return to calmness points to an ending: "Each time, then, the account begins in such a way that one notes a new beginning. And it clearly concludes when the knot has been happily untied. . . . Any competent narrator makes a pause after telling one of these narratives so that the imagination will have time to recover, the hearer may once again reflect upon what has been heard. . . ." (xxviii).

9. Stories in the Latter Prophets or in the Writings are not part of a unified and single sequence.

10. See Trible (1991:170–71) on this opening, in which "[t]he ambiguity of surprise joins the burden of continuation" (171). See also Deurloo 1994b:116.

11. There have been many important and interesting studies devoted to the Akedah story (see Trible 1991:249–50, n. 2), but they are beyond the scope of the present discussion. I mention only Fokkelman's study (1989), which emphasizes the structure and the inclusio.

12. The conception that identifies God as one of the guests and the two others as angels is known from the days of Justin (second century A.D.), see Roberts and Donaldsohn 1867:157–64. See the recent paper by Greenstein 1999:57.

13. The emphasis that Tamar was Absalom's sister convinces most interpreters to assume that Tamar was half-sister of Amnon, meaning that they had a common father but not a common mother. Thus, Tamar's mother was Absalom's mother: "Maacah, daughter of King Talmai of Geshur" (2 Sam 3:3b). According to Reis, Tamar and Amnon had no common parent (1998:44–45).

14. For a brilliant analysis of this opening, see Bar-Efrat 1989:240–45. Trible considers v. 3 to be part of the introduction (1984:37–40).

15. It is a pun on the Hebrew roots *ṣrr* and *yṣr*, which is used to describe lust and passion. Because of these associations and what follows, Trible 1984 prefers to translate and interpret the root "to love" (*ʾhb*) as "to desire" (40). See also p. 38 and her interpretation of v. 1.

16. The other option is to bring the same root (*ḥly*) in the paʿal conjugation, whose meaning is definitely being ill.

17. The first interpretation conforms to the system of cantillation. Ibn-Kaspi 1970:36 discusses the two possibilities.

18. According to Alter 1999, "The last phrase here as a definite negative connotation (rather like the British 'to interfere with her') and makes clear the narrow carnal nature of Amnon's 'love' for Tamar" (265).

19. Conroy 1978:17 pointed to the inclusion between v. 1 and v. 22b.

20. For these boundaries of the story, see Conroy 1978:66–75; Fokkelman 1981:250–51. The boundaries according to Polzin 1993:187–91 are 2 Sam 18:19—19:9a; see also Bar-Efrat 1996b:196–202, who uses 2 Sam 18:19—19:9.

21. Oz states: "All happy families resemble one another; every unhappy family is unhappy in its own fashion. Actually, Tolstoy himself, in *Anna Karenina* and in other works, contradicts this dichotomy" (1991).

22. In the nature of things, the characterization of the serpent ("Now the serpent was the shrewdest of all the wild beasts that the LORD God had made") is a part of the long exposition, whereas the story itself begins in 3:1b.

23. For these boundaries of the story, see Skinner's "The Creation and Fall of Man" (1963:51–90). See also Walsh 1977. Trible 1992:72–143 characterizes Genesis 2–3 as "A Love Story Gone Awry," while her exact boundaries are the same (75, 134ff.). Some divide the same passage into two stories: the story of Eden (2:4b-24) and the fall of Man (2:25—3:24). See Speiser 1964:14–28; similarly Von Rad 1963:71–99. According to Sarna 1989:16–17, the story begins with 2:4a. Rosenberg (1986:47–68; 1992:52–62) focuses on the human life cycle and discovers a collage of cultural themes in the story; his boundaries are 2:4—4:1.

24. For the concentric structure, see Trible 1992:74 and also Rosenberg 1986:47–68.

25. On understanding this opening as the description of a biblical utopia, see Amit 1990.

26. See also Rosenberg 1992: "The story of an expulsion from a paradisic 'Garden' is thus a kind of metaphor, a parable of human maturation" (57).

27. The giving of names means ruling over: see Num 32:38; 2 Kings 23:34; 24:17; 2 Chron 36:4.

5. Plots, Structures, and Their Functions

1. See Baldwin (1963), who follows this five-stage structure from its beginnings with the classical writers to Shakespeare's time. See also Bar-Efrat 1989:94; Fokkelman 1999:15–18, 80–81 and passim. Polak 1994:38–42; 115–20; 214–21) prefers to use the term "pediment." See also n. 28 below.

2. On "telling" and "showing" in biblical stories, see Licht 1978:24–50; Bar-Efrat 1989:93–111 also stresses the scenic character of the plot's units but pays more attention to their symmetric parallel order (see n. 1 above).

3. I say "generally" because there are different cases, too, such as the role of the chorus in ancient Greek dramas or the narrator in Bertolt Brecht's plays.

4. In Hebrew the clause "that Samson had come there" is preceded by the infinitive le'mor ("to say"), indicating direct speech, and may be regarded as a colon. On this infinitive form, see Meier 1992:84–140; Miller 1996:163–212.

5. I might add that direct speech is only one of the ways to create dramatic dimension.

6. For an analysis focusing on the indirections of biblical dialogue and on the use of double entendre in this story, see Sternberg 1991.

7. Compare to Speiser 1964:170. According to Sarna 1989, this expression "is a case of hendiadys, the use of two terms to express a single notion" (158).

8. Also compare to Speiser 1964:170. According to Sarna 1989, "it is

unclear whether this term . . . simply connot[es] the general body of citizens, or whether it refers to a specific entity, meaning the ruling oligarchy," and he adds: "It seems that the support of this group was needed before an alien could acquire real estate and before a citizen would agree to negotiate the sale of his property" (158).

9. Speiser 1964 reads: "sell me a burial site from your holdings . . ." (170), and explains that "the preposition ʿim has here the technical sense of 'under one's authority'" (170).

10. Sarna 1989 says: "It can mean 'to give, sell, pay.' Its many meanings permit the dialogue to be conducted in an atmosphere of delicate and dignified, if somewhat contrived, politeness" (158). See also Gen 25:34; Joel 4:3; Prov 31:24; 1 Kings 21:6.

11. Speiser 1964:170 explains here *nāśîʾ* here as an honorific epithet.

12. Masoretic and Samaritan manuscripts have "upon Mamre" as in v. 19. Skinner 1963 suggests "to the east of" (338); see also Wenham 1994:129.

13. Compare to Sarna 1989:159.

14. Compare to Speiser 1964:171.

15. See also *Gen Rab* 79:7: "three passages on the basis of which the nations of the world cannot ridicule Israel, saying, 'You have stolen property. They are, first, the cave at Machpelah, second, the site of the Temple, and third, the sepulchre of Joseph . . .'" (Neusner 1985:142–43).

16. This story is mentioned above in connection with the insertion made by the editor of the Book of Kings, p. 30.

17. This phrase is intended, as we have seen (see p. 37), to link up the stories and place them in chronological order.

18. The Septuagint lacks the words "in Jezreel," according to Gray (1977:436 note c), because they are tautological after "Naboth the Jezreelite." Gray explains that because of v. 18 this gloss is "an effort on the part of the redactor to clarify the position." It is an open question if the story took place in Jezreel or in Samaria. According to Na'aman (1997:124–25), "the author was unaware of the site of the two towns and hopelessly confused the locations of the palace and vineyard. The glosses in verses 1a and 18a were inserted into the text by an editor in an effort to resolve the difficulties."

19. Compare to Amos 3:15: "I will wreck the winter palace together with the summer palace. . . ."

20. The term *hekal* occurs sixty-nine times concerning God's temple and eleven times concerning a palace. It is interesting to note that these proportions are changed in Aramaic: six times for God's temple and eight times for a foreign king's palace. This word in Akkadian signifies the king's palace,

while in Ugaritic it is a poetic synonym for "house," so that the "house of god" means the "palace of god."

21. See Zakovitch 1984:384.

22. There being no report about where she took the seal and where the letters were written, we do not know if the king had a study close to his bedroom. It is possible to regard vv. 8-10 as a new scene that takes place in a different place; but as it does not state that she left the place in order to get the king's seal, I prefer to assume that it happened in the same surroundings or very nearby.

23. See Exod 22:27: "You shall not revile God, nor put a curse upon a chieftain among your people."

24. This correspondence with the law of Deuteronomy (see also Deut 17:5-7; Num 35:30) has been seen by some scholars as additional proof of the late writing of the story. See Rofé 1988b: "It seems that all four collections of laws—BC, H, D, and P—were already known to the author of our story" (101). But also see Carmichael 1974.

25. A critical approach to the repetitions in v. 11 is to be found in Kittel *BHK* (1937), and see also Gray 1977:437; but according to Montgomery 1951, "the repetitions may be due to legal form" (332).

26. I make no reference to the rest of the prophecy, which has already been discussed as an editorial addition (vv. 20b-26), see above, pp. 30–31.

27. On the possibility that vv. 27-29 reflect a later stage, see Rofé 1988b:95.

28. Some other common symmetrical structures are the ring or envelope structure (A . . . A) and the chiastic structure (A, B, B, A). Kugel 1981 asks: "what's so great about symmetry? . . . or did precise symmetry simply not hold the same attraction for him or for us?" (225); but see Berlin's (1982) response.

29. For other discussions of the structure of this story, see Long 1984:223–27; and Walsh 1996:316–41.

30. Zakovitch 1984:387–88; Walsh 1996:321, 327, 333–34.

31. On the pediment structure in this story, see the first part of chapter 5 above; on its exposition and ending, see pp. 48–49. For a full analysis of this story, its structural units, the gaps and their significance, see Amit 1999a:171–98. Alter (1981:37–41) used this story as an example of historical writing in the Bible, but see the criticism in Amit 1999b:109–14.

32. The size is unknown and is mentioned in the Bible only here. Targum Jonathan translates forearm (some 30 cm. in length). Rashi, who seeks to minimize its length, adds, a short forearm.

33. For a different explanation, see Halpern 1988:39–75.

34. For an extensive discussion of this structure and its different functions, see Zakovitch 1979.

35. See Zakovitch 1979:244–49.

36. Although the terminology "three and four pattern" is not mentioned, this structure appears in the analysis of Bal (1987:49–58), who emphasizes the division into four attempts and even the connection between the third attempt and the fourth. See also Zakovitch 1979:228–33; Amit 1999a: 285–88.

37. Since we know there were five Philistine lords, see 1 Sam 6:4.

38. Zakovitch (1979:xviii–xix, 306–10) defines the case of Job as a "Report of Disaster."

39. For the attempt to describe the structure of this story as a concentric pattern and its criticism, see Conroy 1978:18–20.

40. See Habel 1965, who terms this type of story, "Call Narratives." See also Culley 1976:59–63.

41. Alter (1981:47–62) refers to these story-structures as "type-scenes."

6. Creating Characters with Minimal Means

1. Auerbach (1957), who compared the Homeric style with that of the Hebrew Bible, explained the brevity of the latter as a result of being "permeated with the most unrelieved suspense and directed toward a single goal (and to that extent far more of a unity), remains mysterious and 'fraught with background'" (9).

2. For an analysis of Berlin's characterization, see Alter 1981:116–27.

3. For a different view, which criticizes Berlin, based on subjective feminist reading, see Bach 1990:34.

4. In distinguishing between the public and the private life, Berlin is following Gunn (1978):87–111), who separates David the king from David the man.

5. See the section "Reconstructing Yhwh" in Gunn and Fewell (1993: 81–89): "From a faith position, Jewish or Christian, there are powerful traditional reasons to read for a positively construed, flat character" (85).

6. In order to depict God as a developing character, Miles (1996), who created God's biography, had to treat the Hebrew Bible as a single diachronic story.

7. Berlin 1983:23–33. For different observations on characterization in the Bible, see Bach 1993 and the bibliography there.

8. Nehama Leibowitz (1976) comments thus on the moral problem of this episode: "Strange and inescapable is the fact that Moses first of the

prophets, the lawgiver, began his career by being involved in a killing. This disturbing circumstance has constantly preoccupied commentators ancient and modern" (41). See also pp. 41–46.

9. According to Adar's reading of 1 Sam 13:8-14 (1959:226–27): "A careful study of the episode of the first clash with Samuel reveals the confusion of the narrator himself. . . . The narrator's tendency to see Saul's good side is shown. . . . No doubt this is an example of the narrator's dramatic tendency, but from the way it is formulated we receive the impression that Samuel acted deliberately. . . . The narrator does not justify or condemn Saul, but he sees the force of his arguments and his position, and in any case he does not accuse him of the lust for power; Saul was identifying himself completely with the battle." On this issue, see Gunn (1980:65-67), Fokkelman (1986:37), Miscall (1986:81–89), who emphasizes different readings, and Polzin (1989:129), who emphasizes the part of the narrator in creating a picture "of a laudable and credible Saul." See also Exum (1992:27–28), and similarly, Alter (1999), who suspects Samuel and describes him as interested in "setting him [Saul] up for failure by arriving at an arranged rendezvous at the last possible moment" (xvi).

10. Segal (1956:232) was one of the first to suspect the Amalekite; see also Hertzberg 1972:237; Gunn 1980:157 n. 21; Conroy 1983:91; Berlin 1983:80; Fokkelman (1986:640ff.); and lately Polzin 1993:2–8; Reinhartz 1998:56–59. See also pp. 96–99 above.

11. See also Noll (1997:), who asks: "Is this the self-serving opportunist speaking, who eulogizes his former enemies for propagandistic purposes? Or is this the more humane side of David speaking?" (116).

12. It may be noted here that the first condition of the pact between Abner and David was the return of Michal to David. In other words, this was a practical arrangement in which David regained his link to the house of Saul, with its legitimation of his monarchy, and Abner avenged himself against Ishbosheth and regained his position in David's court (2 Sam 3:6-21).

13. See Gunn 1980: "For present purposes, however, I am content to observe that it can be both moving and ironical" (157 n. 22). Polzin (1993: 10–14) is aware of David's political motivation.

14. I first discussed this issue in an article (Amit 1987), which underwent changes in its Hebrew version (1993).

15. Mostly in Deuteronomy and the Deuteronomistic school.

16. Compare to Greenstein 1999.

17. It is worth noting that the figure of Samson was changed in later literature and in art, and we may assume that it was different in the pre-biblical stage. See Fishlov 2000.

18. See Zakovitch 1982 and Amit 1999a:266–309 and the additional bibliography there.

19. Most commentators since the nineteenth century have divided this cycle into two parts, with the point of division in Judges 8:4. For a bibliography on this subject, and other proposed divisions, including a detailed discussion of the present suggestion, see Amit 1999a: 229, n. 15, as well as pp. 232–47.

20. See Rofé 1988b. For a different view, see Pippin 1994 (including her bibliography) and, more recently, Walsh 1996:316–41. See also Stanton 1999: part 2, 74, and the attempt to do Jezebel justice by Ellen Battelle Dietrick (in Stanton 1999: part 2, 74–76).

21. As to the place of vv. 20b-26, see chapter 3 above and the discussion on literal criticism, pp. 30–31.

22. On the criteria for determining the leading character, see Sternberg 1970:499–508. On the applications of his criteria to biblical narrative, see Amit 1999a:214–18. See Walsh 1996:327–28 for a discussion about the main characters in this story.

23. See also Trible 1984:36–63. For a different view that blames Tamar, see Reis 1998.

24. Author's translation of Hebrew.

25. See Amit (1983) on 2 Sam 13:1-22 as a story of sympathy for Absalom. Conroy (1978:102–3; 1983:118–21) states that there is no indication that Absalom hated Amnon as a rival for the throne. According to Conroy, "Political consequences should not be confused with political motivation," and this case should be seen as a "personal, non-political matter" (1978:103).

26. Both early and late commentators present Judah in a bad light. An examination of the early ones, with broad acceptance of their view, is found in Shinan and Zakovitch 1992. Alter's interpretation (1981:3–12) also remains faithful to the traditional one. Gunn and Fewell's (1993:34–45) focus on Tamar's victory inevitably reflects badly on Judah. But see Bal's (1987:89–103, especially p. 90) criticism of Alter. She is aware of the chronological break but is more interested in the editor's motivation for putting the three chapters [37–39] in a sequence. For a different view of Judah, see Amit 2000:79–83.

27. On Tamar as the "woman who brings death," see Blenkinsopp (1966: 52–53), and as a symbol of the "killer wife" superstition, see Friedman 1990.

28. According to Niditch, verse 27b "may be the editorial comment of a later Priestly redactor, concerned that Judah not consciously ignore the incest taboo of Lev. 18:15" (1979:14). But if the whole story is late, it might be original and an attempt to fit the norms of the audience and depict Judah in a positive light.

29. For more allusions to David throughout this story, see Blenkinsopp 1966:53; and Greenstein 1990:165–66.

7. Whom to Believe?

1. There has been a recent tendency to depict God as a liar and a deceiver (Horn Prouser 1991:143–69), who deals mostly with biblical narrative. To my mind, her examples (Gen 2:17; 18:13; 1 Kings 22:19-23) are not convincing.

2. For this comparison, see Chatman 1978:143–61.

3. For some additional possibilities and a preference for the second, see Cassuto 1961:124–25.

4. For an examination of early and late commentators, see Amit 1985:92–96; and see above pp. 78–79 and the quotation from Moshe Zvi Segal there.

5. For a detailed examination of these verses and additional textual differences, see Amit 1985:97–99.

6. The Chronicler uses the wordplay of Josh 7:25–26 and the name of the place, "Valley of Trouble."

7. On the different solutions for this discrepancy, see Amit 1992.

8. The Biblical Story and the Use of Time

1. Lessing, under the term "painting," includes "the plastic arts in general"; while under the term "poetry," he claims the right to include "those other arts in which the method of imitation [namely, presentation in time] is progressive" (1895:6).

2. For a fairly recent and full discussion on the aspect of time, see Ricoeur 1985 and Genette 1994.

3. For a detailed examination of Judges 1 as part of the exposition to the Book of Judges, see Amit 1999a:141–52 and also O'Connell 1996:59–70.

4. This accords with Genesis: "and they shall be enslaved and oppressed four hundred years" (15:13).

5. See also Judg 5:31b; 8:28b; 10:2, 3; as well as 1 Sam 4:18b; 2 Sam 5:4-5; and many more.

6. Conroy emphasizes that the time markers help "to explain changes in character" (1978:106–8).

7. On the hidden polemic in the incident of the concubine in Gibeah as implying a character assassination of Saul, see Amit 2000:167–88, esp. 178–88.

8. On the additional use of repetition, see, for example, Sternberg 1985: 365–440.

9. See Leibowitz 1972:230–38.

10. See Weiss 1965:181–206 (especially pp. 202–3).

11. Rimmon-Kenan 1983:48. The explanations in brackets are my own.

12. See Sarna 1981.

13. See Amit 2000:224–40, and also the extensive bibliography there.

9. Place, Story, and History

1. This chapter is mostly based on my article, "The Function of Topographical Indications in the Biblical Story (Amit 1985–1987).

2. See Simon 1961 and Brinkman 1992.

3. "The linear structure of the text gives greater dominance to the time dimension of the world. While it has by no means the exclusive status of an autocrat, as Lessing thought, in the final analysis it remains undisputed" (Zoran 1997:76). For additional bibliography, see his book.

4. Twelve pages (less than 5 percent) are devoted to the issue of space (Bar-Efrat 1989:184–96). Polak (1994) almost ignores the subject, and Fokkelman, who devotes a chapter to "Time and Space, Entrances and Exits" (1999:97–111), although he is more interested in the presentation of parallel symmetries, mentions explicit indications of time and space—mostly together—accompanied by verbs of movement.

5. Even Alter, who analyzes the story from a literary point of view, concludes: "It is perhaps less historicized fiction than fictionalized history— history in which the feeling and the meaning of events are concretely realized through the technical resources of prose fiction" (1981:41). According to Halpern, who focuses on the palace: "This is history, historical narrative, intended to be reenactment to communicate antiquarian data" (1994:68).

6. Josephus, *Jewish Antiquities,* 5.188–96. It is noteworthy that most scholars follow his interpretation, lately Halpern (1994:40).

7. While most commentators follow Deut 34:3 and 2 Chron 28:15 in identifying "the City of Palms" with Jericho, *Mishnah Yebamoth* 16:7 identifies it with Zoar. For the diverse identifications and their history, see Aharoni 1971.

8. On the identification of these places and the relation of literature versus history in the story of the victory in the days of Deborah, see Amit 1999a:198–221.

9. In Hebrew, the name *Uz* suggests the root *'ws* and the noun *'sh*, which hint at wisdom literature—that is, the genre to which the Book of Job belongs—and may thus imply the author's deliberate choice. Thus already Rashi, and see also Weiss 1983:23–24, and there note 6.

10. On the problems concerning the identification of these places, see any commentary on the Book of Job, as, for example, Pope 1965:3–5, 23–24; Habel 1985:86, 97.

11. See Cassuto 1961:114–21. On page 118 he emphasizes that the description of the rivers tells us that, according to the Torah, the Garden of Eden was not situated in our world.

12. On Chronicles as ideological writing and on the relation to the siege of Sennacherib, see Japhet 1989:372 and especially n. 69.

13. See Gunkel (1997:xviii, xxff.), who discusses the ritual background of those places.

14. Cassuto also sees a parallel between the events depicted in the Book of Genesis and the conquests of Joshua (1964:303–6; 322–25). See also Deurloo 1994a.

15. See Cassuto 1964:336–37.

16. See Myers 1965:9.

17. See Talmon 1966.

18. Compare with the story of the ark in 1 Sam 5:1—6:12, for example; and see Amit 2000:46ff. and the additional bibliography there.

19. This concept was no doubt influenced by Mesopotamian myths about the struggles of *Tiamat,* the goddess of the primeval world-ocean against the creative God, as well as by Canaanite myths about the battles of Baal with the lord of the sea, which infiltrated into Israelite culture. See Isa 51:9-10, among others; and Cassuto 1961:8–12, 23–25, 36–38, 49–51; Cassuto 1972a; and Day 1985.

20. The only character who is named in this story is Phinehas son of Eleazar son of Aaron (Judg 20:28). Critical commentators hold that this was an insertion. See Amit 2000:179, and there n. 29.

21. On the story of the concubine of Gibeah as an implicit polemic against Saul, see Amit 2000:178–88.

10. Inherent and Added Significance

1. For the detailed analysis, see Conroy 1978 and especially pp. 23–24, 100, 111; See also Amit 1983. The sympathy for Absalom will serve as preparation for subsequent events.

2. This loaded exposition was discussed in detail on pp. 39–40 above.

3. Halpern (1988:52–54) analyzes the architectural data of Amnon's house.

4. The context convinces Conroy (1978:25) that Tamar went to Absalom's house immediately after her expulsion by Amnon.

5. For an extensive discussion and bibliography, see Bohlen 1978.

6. See Rofé 1988b and additional bibliography there.

7. Zakovitch 1984. Rofé 1988b:94 (see also n. 20 there) objects to the preference for this message and asks: "If this was intended, could it have been done implicitly and concomitantly only?"

8. See also Walsh 1996:316–41. He calls vv. 17–29 "Prophetic Condemnation."

9. See 1 Kings 18:4; 19:1-2.

10. Compare Greenstein 1998.

11. See Walsh (1996): "The royal house undermines the very structure of social stability it has the obligation to uphold" (327). Walsh also emphasizes "the royal couple's assault on the legal and religious principles that guarantee the structure of Israelite society" (326).

11. The Story and Its Contexts

1. On the parts that create the biblical historiography, see Amit 1999b.

2. For a discussion of the place of the Book of Samuel in the deuteronomistic ideology and the Chronicler's approach, see Amit 1999b:42–48, 56–64, and 82–98, as well as the bibliography there.

3. According to Rofé (1988a:44-51), 2 Kings 2:1-18, which is usually called "The Ascension of Elijah," forms the opening section of Elisha cycle.

4. These two issues, the lateness and 2 Kings 9:25-26, are dealt with at length by Rofé 1988b:95–101.

5. See Japhet 1989:153–54; Amit 1999b:56–64.

6. According to Skinner (1963:450), the story belongs to J and the editor is R[JE] (the redactor of J and E).

7. This technique was first discovered by Kuhl (1952), who called it *Wideraufnahme*. Today we know that the same technique could serve both the editors and the original writers to expand the subject, see Polak 1994:77–80.

8. Compare Ibn Ezra: "That is not the time when Joseph was sold, but before it happened." See also Shinan and Zakovitch 1992:207. On the editor's purpose in setting this story exactly here, see Goldin 1977:43–44. For a different view, see Emerton, who argues that Genesis 38 "never stood

anywhere but between the accounts of the selling of Joseph into slavery and the doings of Joseph in Egypt in that source" (1975:360).

9. See Cassuto 1972b:109–10; Goldin 1977:28–29; and lately the discussion in Alter (1981:3–12), who seeks to stress the difference between his approach and that of the Sages.

10. It is generally agreed that the Book of Chronicles is late. Opinions are divided about the date of the Book of Ruth, while there is a growing consensus to set it late. See Sasson (1979:240–52), who claims "that the reign of Josiah (640–609 B.C.E.) might well have provided a setting in which Ruth, a folktale, became a vehicle for the glorification of David" (251). He is cautious about dating its actual writing yet sets it in approximately the middle of the fifth century B.C.E. Zakovitch maintains that the Book of Ruth is late (1990:14–35).

11. On the fine, and sometimes vague, boundary between the author and the editor, see Amit 1999a:1–24.

Afterword

1. We have touched only briefly on these issues since they lead to another subject that deserves a book of its own, namely, the art of editing in the Hebrew Bible.

Works Cited

Adar, Zvi. 1959. *The Biblical Narrative.* Jerusalem: Department of the Jewish Agency for Israel, Goldberg's Press.

Aharoni, Yohanan. 1971. "The City of Palms." *EB* 6:218 (Jerusalem: Bialik Institute) [Heb.].

Alonso-Schökel, Luis. 1961. "Erzählkunst im Buche der Richter." *Bib* 42:143–72.

Alter, Robert. 1981. *The Art of Biblical Narrative.* New York: Basic Books.

―――. 1990. "Samson without Folklore." In *Text and Tradition: The Hebrew Bible and Folklore,* ed. Susan Niditch, 47–56. Atlanta: Scholars Press.

―――. 1999. *The David Story: A Translation with Commentary of 1 and 2 Samuel.* New York: Norton.

Amit, Yairah. 1983. "The Story of Amnon and Tamar: Reservoir of Sympathy for Absalom." *Hasifrut/Literature* 32:80–87 [Heb.].

―――. 1985. "Three Variations on the Death of Saul: Studies in the Fashioning of the World, in Reliability and in the Tendentiousness of Biblical Narrative." *BM* 100.1:92–102 [Heb.].

―――. 1985–87. "The Function of Topographical Indications in the Biblical Story." In *Shnaton: An Annual for Biblical and Ancient Near Eastern Studies,* ed. M. Weinfeld, 9:15–30. Jerusalem and Tel Aviv: M. Newman.

―――. 1987. "The Dual Causality Principle and Its Effects on Biblical Literature." *VT* 37:385–400.

————. 1989. "The Multi-Purpose 'Leading Word' and the Problems of Its Usage." *Proof* 9:99–114.

————. 1990. "Biblical Utopianism: A Mapmakers Guide to Eden." *USQR* 44:11–17.

————. 1992. "'The Glory of Israel Does Not Deceive or Change His Mind': On the Reliability of Narrator and Speakers in Biblical Narrative." *Proof* 12:201–12.

————. 1993. "Dual Causality: An Additional Aspect." *BM* 132.1: 41–55 [Heb.].

————. 1997. "Creation and the Calendar of Holiness." In *Tehillah le-Moshe: Biblical and Judaic Studies in Honor of Moshe Greenberg*, ed. M. Cogan, B. L. Eichler, J. H. Tigay, 13–29. Winona Lake, Ind.: Eisenbrauns [Heb.].

————. 1999a. *The Book of Judges: The Art of Editing*. Trans. J. Chipman. BibIntSer 38. Leiden: Brill.

————. 1999b. *History and Ideology: An Introduction to Historiography in the Hebrew Bible*. Trans. Y. Lotan. BibIntSer 60. Sheffield: Sheffield Academic Press.

————. 2000. *Hidden Polemics in Biblical Narrative*. Trans. J. Chipman. BibIntSer 25. Leiden: Brill.

Aristotle. 1970. *Poetics*. Trans. with an intro. and notes by Gerald F. Else. Ann Arbor, Mich.: Univ. of Michigan Press.

Arpali, Boaz. 1970. "Caution, A Biblical Story! Comments on the Story of David and Bathsheba and on the Problems of Biblical Narrative." *Hasifrut/Literature* 2:580–97 [Heb.].

Auerbach, Erich. 1957 (1946). *Mimesis: The Representation of Reality in Western Literature*. Trans. W. Trask. Garden City, N.Y.: Doubleday.

Bach, Alice. 1990. "The Pleasure of Her Text." In *The Pleasure of Her Text: Feminist Readings of Biblical and Historical Texts,* ed. Alice Bach, 25–44. Philadelphia: Trinity Press International.

————. 1993. "Signs of the Flesh: Observations on Characterization in the Bible." *Semeia* 63:61–70.

Bal, Mieke. 1987. *Lethal Love: Feminist Literary Readings of Biblical Love Stories*. ISBL. Bloomington: Indiana Univ. Press.

————. 1991. "The Bible as Literature." In *On Story-Telling: Essays in Narratology,* ed. D. Jobling, 59–72. Sonoma, Calif.: Polebridge.

Baldwin, Thomas Whitfield. [1947] 1963. *William Shakespeare's Five-Act Structure*. Urbana: Univ. of Illinois Press.

Bar-Efrat, Shimeon. 1989. *Narrative Art in the Bible*. Trans. D. Shefer-Vanson. Sheffield: Almond.

————. 1996a. *I Samuel*. Miqra le-Yisrael. Tel Aviv: Am Oved, Jerusalem: Magnes Press [Heb.].

———. 1996b. *II Samuel*. Miqra le-Yisrael. Tel Aviv: Am Oved, Jerusalem: Magnes Press [Heb.].

Berlin, Adele. 1982. "On the Bible as Literature." *Proof* 2:323–27.

———. 1983. *Poetics and Interpretation of Biblical Narrative*. BLS 9. Sheffield: Almond.

Blenkinsopp, Joseph. 1966. "Theme and Motif in the Succession History (2 Sam xi 2ff) and the Yahwist Corpus." In *Volume du Congrès: Genève 1965*, 44–57. VTSup 15. Leiden: Brill.

Bohlem, Reinhold. 1978. *Der Fall Nabot: Form, Hintergrund und Werdegang einer altte alttestamentlichen Erzälung (1 Kön. 21)*. TTZ 35. Trier: Paulinus.

Brinkman, Johan Marie. 1992. *The Perception of Space in the Old Testament: An Exploration of the Methodological Problems of Its Investigation, Exemplified by a Study of Exodus 25 to 31*. Kampen, Netherlands: Kok Pharos.

Brown, Francis, S. R. Driver, Charles A. Briggs. 1907. *A Hebrew and English Lexicon of the Old Testament*. Based on Wilhelm Gesenius. Trans. E. Robinson. Oxford: Clarendon.

Buber, Martin. 1994a [1927]. "Leitwort Style in Pentateuch Narrative." In *Scripture and Translation: Martin Buber and Franz Rosenzweig*, trans. L. Rosenwald with E. Fox, 114–28. Bloomington: Indiana Univ. Press.

———. 1994b [1935]. "Leitwort and Discourse Type." In *Scripture and Translation: Martin Buber and Franz Rosenzweig*, trans. L. Rosenwald with E. Fox, 143–50. Bloomington: Indiana Univ. Press.

Carmichael, Calum M. 1974. *The Laws of Deuteronomy*. Ithaca: Cornell Univ. Press.

Cassuto, Umberto. 1961. *A Commentary on the Book of Genesis, Part I: From Adam to Noah, Genesis I–VI 8*. Trans. I Abrahams. Jerusalem: Magnes Press [Heb.].

———. 1964. *A Commentary on the Book of Genesis, Part II: From Noah to Abraham, Genesis VI9–XI32*. Trans. I Abrahams. Jerusalem: Magnes Press [Heb.].

———. 1972a. "The Israelite Epic." In *Biblical and Canaanite Literatures: Studies on the Bible and Ancient Orient*, vol. 1, 62–90. Jerusalem: Magnes Press [Heb.].

———. 1972b. "The Story of Tamar and Judah." In *Biblical and Canaanite Literatures: Studies on the Bible and Ancient Orient*, vol. 1, 109–17. Jerusalem: Magnes Press [Heb.].

Chatman, Seymour. 1978. *Story and Discourse: Narrative Structure in Fiction and Film*. Ithaca, N.Y.: Cornell Univ. Press.

Conroy, Charles. 1978. *Absalom, Absalom!: Narrative and Language in 2 Sam 13—20*. AnBib 81. Rome: Biblical Institute.

————. 1983. *1–2 Samuel, 1–2 Kings: With an Excursus on Davidic Dynasty and Holy City Zion.* Wilmington, Del.: Michael Glazier.

Culley, Robert C. 1963. "An Approach to the Problem of Oral Tradition." *VT* 13:113–25.

————. 1976. *Studies in the Structure of Hebrew Narrative.* SemSt. Philadelphia: Fortress Press; Missoula, Mont.: Scholars Press.

Day, John. 1985. *God's Conflict with the Dragon and the Sea: Echoes of a Canaanite Myth in the Old Testament.* University of Cambridge Oriental Publications 35. Cambridge: Cambridge Univ. Press.

Deem, Ariella. 1979. "'Cupboard Love': The Story of Amnon and Tamar." *Hasifrut/Literature* 28:100–107 [Heb.].

Deurloo, K. A. 1994a. "The Way of Abraham." In *Voices from Amsterdam: A Modern Tradition of Reading Biblical Narrative,* ed. M. Kessler, 95–112. SemSt. Atlanta: Scholars Press.

————. 1994b. "'Because You Have Hearkened to My Voice': Genesis 22." In *Voices from Amsterdam: A Modern Tradition of Reading Biblical Narrative,* ed. M. Kessler, 113–30. SemSt. Atlanta: Scholars Press.

Driver, S. R. 1913a [1891]. *An Introduction to the Literature of the Old Testament.* ITL. Edinburgh: T. & T. Clark.

————. 1913b [1889]. *Notes on the Hebrew Text and the Topography of the Books of Samuel.* Oxford: Clarendon.

Emerton, John A. 1975. "Some Problems in Genesis XXXVIII." *VT* 25:338–60.

Ewen, Josef. 1980. *Character in Narrative.* Israel: Sifriyat Hapoalim [Heb.].

Exum, J. Cheryl. 1976. "Literary Patterns in the Samson Saga: An Investigation of Rhetorical Style in Biblical Prose." Ph.D. diss., Columbia Univ.

————. 1992. *Tragedy and Biblical Narrative: Arrows of the Almighty.* Cambridge: Cambridge Univ. Press.

Fishelov, David. 2000. *Samson's Locks: The Transformation of Biblical Samson.* Tel Aviv: Haifa Univ. Press and Zmora-Bitan [Heb.].

Fokkelman, Jan P. 1981. *Narrative Art and Poetry in the Books of Samuel: A Full Interpretation Based on Stylistic and Structural Analyses.* Vol. I: *King David (II Sam 9–20 & I Kings 1–2).* SSN 20. Assen, Netherlands: Van Gorcum.

————. 1986. *Narrative Art and Poetry in the Books of Samuel,* Vol. II: *The Crossing Fates (I Sam 13–31&II Sam 1).* SSN 23. Assen, Netherlands: Van Gorcum.

————. 1989. "'On the Mount of the Lord There Is Vision': A Response to Francis Landy Concerning the Akedah." In *Signs and Wonders: Biblical Texts in Literary Focus,* ed. J. C. Exum, 41–57. SemSt. Atlanta: Scholars Press.

————. 1999. *Reading Biblical Narrative: A Practical Guide.* Trans. I. Smit. Leiden: Deo; Louisville: Westminster John Knox.

Forster, E. M. 1949 [1927]. *Aspects of the Novel.* London: Edward Arnold.

Friedman, Mordechai Akiva. 1990. "Tamar, a Symbol of Life: The 'Killer Wife' Superstition in the Bible and Jewish Tradition." *AJSR* 15:23–61.

Garsiel, Moshe. 1977. "The Story of Ehud Son of Gera (Judges 3:12-30)." In *Reflections on Scripture: Selections from Studies of the Yishai Ron Memorial Bible Circle* II, 57–77. Tel Aviv: Don. Expanded version: 1971. "The Story of Ehud Son of Gera in the Book of Judges." *BM* 46.3:285–92.

Genette, Gérard. 1994 [1983]. *Narrative Discourse Revisited.* Trans. J. E. Lewin; Ithaca, N.Y.: Cornell Univ. Press.

Goldin, Judah. 1977. "The Youngest Son or Where Does Genesis 38 Belong?" *JBL* 96:27–44.

Gray, John. 1977 [1964]. *I & II Kings: A Commentary.* OTL. London: SCM; Philadelphia: Westminster.

Greenstein, Edward L. 1989. "Deconstruction and Biblical Narrative." *Proof* 9:43–71.

————. 1990. "The Formation of the Biblical Narrative Corpus." *AJSR.* 15:151–78.

————. 1998. "Reading Strategies and the Story of Ruth." In *Women in the Hebrew Bible: A Reader,* ed. A. Bach, 211–31. London: Routledge.

————. 1999. "The God of Israel and the Gods of Canaan: How Different Were They?" In *Proceedings of the Twelfth World Congress of Jewish Studies, Division A: The Bible and Its World.* Jerusalem: World Union of Jewish Studies, Magnes Press.

Gunkel, Hermann. 1997 [1910]. *Genesis.* Trans. M. E. Biddle. MLBS. Macon, Ga.: Mercer Univ. Press.

Gunn, David M. 1978. *The Story of King David: Genre and Interpretation.* JSOTSup 6. Sheffield: Dept. of Biblical Studies, Univ. of Sheffield.

————. 1980. *The Fate of King Saul: An Interpretation of a Biblical Story.* JSOTSup 14. Sheffield: JSOT Press.

Gunn, David M., and Danna Nolan Fewell. 1993. *Narrative in the Hebrew Bible.* OBS. New York: Oxford Univ. Press.

Habel, Norman C. 1965. "The Form and Significance of the Call Narratives." *ZAW* 77:297–323.

————. 1985. *The Book of Job.* OTL. London: SCM; Philadelphia: Westminster.

Halpern, Baruch. 1988. *The First Historians: The Hebrew Bible and History.* San Francisco: Harper & Row.

Harrington, Daniel J. 1985. "Pseudo-Philo." In *The Old Testament Pseude-pigrapha*, vol. 2, ed. J. H. Charlesworth. Garden City, N.Y.: Doubleday.

Hayes, John H., ed. 1974. *Old Testament Form Criticism*. TUMSR 2. San Antonio: Trinity Univ. Press.

Hertzberg, Hans Wilhelm. 1972 [1960]. *I & II Samuel*. Trans. J. S. Bowden. OTL. Philadelphia: Westminster.

Horn Prouser, Ora. 1991. "The Phenomenology of the Lie in Biblical Narrative." Ph.D. diss., Jewish Theological Seminary of America.

Hurowitz, Victor. 1992. *I Have Built You an Exalted House: Temple Building in the Bible in Light of Mesopotamian and North-West Semitic Writings*. ASORMS 5; JSOTSup 115. Sheffield: JSOT.

Ibn-Kaspi, Joseph. 1970 [1911]. *Adne Keseph: Commentar zu den prophetischen Büchern der heiligen Schrift;* I Heft: *Josua, Richter, Samuel, Konige, Iesaia*. Jerusalem: MAKOR.

Japhet, Sara. 1989. *The Ideology of the Book of Chronicles and Its Place in Biblical Thought*. Trans. A. Barber. BEATAJ 9. Frankfurt: Peter Lang.

Josephus. 1977. *Jewish Antiquities*. Books 5–8. Trans. H. St. J. Thackeray and R. Marcus. LCL. Cambridge: Harvard Univ. Press.

Kittel, Rudolf, ed. 1937. *Biblia Hebraica*. Stuttgart: Württembergische Bibelanstalt.

Krouse, F. Michael. 1949. *Milton's Samson and the Christian Tradition*. Princeton: Princeton Univ. Press.

Kugel, James L. 1981. "On the Bible and Literary Criticism." *Proof* 1:217–36.

———. 1982. "On the Bible and Literary Criticism." *Proof* 1:328–32.

Kuhl, Curt. 1952. "Die Wiederaufnahme: ein Literarkritisches Prinzip?" *ZAW* 64:1–11.

Leibowitz, Nehama. 1972. *Studies in Genesis: In the Context of Ancient and Modern Jewish Bible Commentary*. Trans. A. Newnan. Jerusalem: World Zionist Organization, Dept. for Torah Education and Culture, 1972 [Heb. 1967].

———. 1976. *Studies in Shemot: In the Context of Ancient and Modern Jewish Bible Commentary*. Trans. A. Newnan. Jerusalem: World Zionist Organization, Dept. for Torah Education and Culture [Heb. 1970].

Lessing, Gotthold Ephraim. 1895 [1766]. "Laocoon; or, On the Limits of Painting and Poetry." In *The Laocoon; and Other Prose Writings of Lessing*, ed. and trans. W. B. Ronnfeldt. London: Walter Scott.

Licht, Jacob. 1978. *Storytelling in the Bible*. Jerusalem: Magnes Press.

Long, Burke O. 1976. "Recent Field Studies in Oral Literature and Their Bearing on OT Criticism." *VT* 26:187–98.

———. 1984. *I Kings*. FOTL 9. Grand Rapids, Mich.: Eerdmans.

McCarter, P. Kyle, Jr. 1983 [1980]. *I Samuel*. AB 8. Garden City, N.Y.: Doubleday.

Meier, Samuel A. 1992. *Speaking of Speaking: Marking Direct Discourse in the Hebrew Bible*. VTSup 46. Leiden: Brill.

Melamed, Ezra Zion. 1975. *Bible Commentators*. Jerusalem: Magnes Press [Heb.].

Miles, Jack. 1996. *God: A Biography*. New York: Knopf.

Miller, Cynthia L. 1996. *The Representation of Speech in Biblical Hebrew Narrative: A Linguistic Analysis*. HSM 55. Atlanta: Scholars Press.

Miscall, Peter D. 1986. *1 Samuel: A Literary Reading*. ISBL. Bloomington: Indiana Univ. Press.

Moore, George Foot. 1966 [1895]. *Judges*. ICC. Edinburgh: T. & T. Clark.

Muilenburg, James. 1953. "A Study in Hebrew Rhetoric: Repetition and Style." In *Congress Volume: Copenhagen 1953*, 97–111. VTSup 1. Leiden: Brill, 1953.

Myers, Jacob M. 1965. *Ezra–Nehemiah*. AB 14. Garden City, N.Y.: Doubleday.

Na'aman, Nadav. 1990. "The 'Conquest of Canaan' in Joshua and in History." In *From Nomadism to Monarchy: Archaeological and Historical Aspects of Early Israel*, ed. N. Na'aman, I. Finkelstein, 284–347. Jerusalem: Yad Izhak Ben Zvi, Israel Exploration Society [Heb.] Eng. Trans. 1994.

———. 1997. "Historical and Literary Notes on the Excavation of Tel Jezreel." *TA* 24:122–28.

Neusner, Jacob. 1985. *Genesis Rabbah: The Judaic Commentary to the Book of Genesis, A New American Translation*. Vol. 3. BJS 106. Atlanta: Scholars Press.

Nielsen, Edward. 1954. *Oral Tradition: A Modern Problem in the Old Testament Introduction*. SBT 1/11. London: SCM.

Niditch, Susan. 1979. "The Wronged Woman Righted: An Analysis of Genesis 38." *HTR* 72:143–49.

———. 1996. *Oral World and Written Word: Ancient Israelite Literature*. Library of Ancient Israel. Louisville: Westminster John Knox.

Noll, K. L. 1997. *The Faces of David*. JSOTSup 242. Sheffield: Sheffield Academic Press.

Noth, Martin. 1981. *The Deuteronomistic History*. Trans. J. Doull et al. JSOTSup 15. Sheffield: JSOT.

O'Connell, Robert H. 1996. *The Rhetoric of the Book of Judges*. VTSup 63. Leiden: Brill.

Oz, Amos. 1999. *The Story Begins: Essays on Literature*. Trans. M. Bar-Tura. New York: Harcourt Brace [Heb. 1996].

Perry, Menahem, and Meir Sternberg. 1968. "The King through Ironic Eyes: The Narrator's Devices in the Biblical Story of David and Bathsheba and Two Excurses on the Theory of Narrative Text." *Hasifrut/Literature* 1:263–92 [Heb.].

—————. 1970. "Caution: A Literary Text! Problems in the Poetics and Interpretation of Biblical Narrative." *Hasifrut/Literature* 2:608–63 [Heb.].

Pippin, Tina. 1994. "Jezebel Re-Vamped." In *A Feminist Companion to Samuel and Kings,* 196–206. FCB 5. Sheffield: Sheffield Academic Press.

Polak, Frank. 1994. *Biblical Narrative: Aspects of Art and Design.* Jerusalem: Bialik Institute [Heb.].

Polzin, Robert. 1989. *Samuel and the Deuteronomist: A Literary Study of the Deuteronomic History.* Part 2, *1 Samuel.* San Francisco: Harper & Row.

—————. 1993. *David and the Deuteronomist: A Literary Study of the Deuteronomic History.* Part 3, *2 Samuel.* Bloomington: Indiana Univ. Press.

Pope, Marvin H. 1965. *Job.* AB 15. Garden City, N.Y.: Doubleday.

Rad, Gerhard von. 1956 [1948]. *Studies in Deuteronomy.* Trans. D. M. G. Stalker. SBT 1/9. London: SCM.

—————. 1963 [1956]. *Genesis.* OTL. Trans. J. H. Marks. London: SCM; Philadelphia: Westminster.

Reinhartz, Adele. 1998. *"Why Ask My Name?": Anonymity and Identity in Biblical Narrative.* New York: Oxford Univ. Press.

Reis, Pamela Tamarkin. 1998. "Cupidity and Stupidity: Woman's Agency and the 'Rape' of Tamar." *JANESCU* 25:43–60.

Ricoeur, Paul. 1984– . *Time and Narrative.* 3 vols. Trans. K. M. McLaughlin and D. Pellauer. Chicago : Univ. of Chicago Press.

Rimmon-Kenan, Shlomith. 1983. *Narrative Fiction: Contemporary Poetics.* New York: Methuen.

Roberts, A. and J. Donaldsohn, eds. 1867. *The Writings of Justin Martyr and Athenagoras.* Vol. 2. Trans. M. Dodds et al. Edinburgh: Ante-Nicene Christian Library.

Robertson, David. 1976. "The Bible as Literature." In *IDBSup,* 547–51. Nashville: Abingdon.

Rofé, Alexander. 1986. "Methodological Aspects of the Study of Biblical Law." In *Jewish Law Association Studies: The Jerusalem Conference Volume,* ed. B. S. Jackson, 1–16. Atlanta: Scholars Press.

—————. 1988a [1982]. *The Prophetical Stories: The Narratives about the Prophets in the Hebrew Bible, Their Literary Types and History.* Trans. D. Levy. Jerusalem: Magnes Press.

————. 1988b. "The Vineyard of Naboth: The Origin and Message of the Story." *VT* 38:89–104.

Rosenberg, Joel. 1986. *King and Kin: Political Allegory in the Hebrew Bible.* ISBL. Bloomington: Indiana Univ. Press.

————. 1992 [1984]. "Biblical Narrative." In *Back to the Sources: Reading the Classic Jewish Texts,* ed. B. W. Holtz, 31–81. New York: Summit.

Rosenzweig, Franz. 1994. "The Secret of Biblical Narrative Form." In *Scripture and Translation,* Martin Buber and Franz Rosenzweig, 129–42. Trans. L. Rosenwald with E. Fox. ISBL. Bloomington: Indiana Univ. Press.

Ryken, Leland. 1984. *How to Read the Bible as Literature.* Grand Rapids: Zondervan.

Sarna, Nahum M. 1981. "The Anticipatory Use of Information as a Literary Feature of the Genesis Narratives." In *The Creation of Sacred Literature: Composition and Reduction of the Biblical Text,* 76–82. Near Eastern Studies 22, ed. R. E. Friedman. Berkeley: Univ. of California Press.

————. 1989. *Genesis.* JPS Torah Commentary. Philadelphia: JPS.

Sasson, Jack M. 1989. *Ruth: A New Translation with a Philological Commentary and a Formalist-Folklorist Interpretation.* BibSem Sheffield: JSOT.

Segal, Moshe Zvi. 1956. *The Books of Samuel.* Jerusalem: Kiryat Sepher [Heb.].

The Septuagint Version of the Old Testament with an English Translation and with Various Readings and Critical Notes. 1879. New York: Harper and Brothers.

Shinan, Avigdor, and Yair Zakovitch. 1992. *The Story of Judah and Tamar: Genesis 38 in the Bible, the Old Versions and the Ancient Jewish Literature.* Research Projects of the Institute of Jewish Studies Monograph Series 15. Jerusalem: Hebrew Univ. [Heb.].

Simon, Uriel. 1961. "Time and Space in Biblical Thinking." Ph.D. diss. Hebrew Univ.

————. 1970. "An Ironic Approach to a Bible Story: On the Interpretation of the Story of David and Bathsheba." *Hasifrut/Literature* 2:598–607 [Heb.].

————. 1997. *Reading Prophetic Narratives.* Trans. L. J. Schramm. ISBL. Bloomington: Indiana Univ. Press.

Skinner, John. 1963 [1910, 1930]. *Genesis.* ICC. Edinburgh: T. & T. Clark.

Soggin, J. Alberto. 1981. *Judges.* OTL. Trans. J. Bowden. Philadelphia: Westminster.

Speiser, E. A. 1964. *Genesis.* AB 1. Garden City, N.Y.: Doubleday.

Stanton, Elizabeth Cady. 1999 [1895–98]. *The Woman's Bible.* Great Minds Series. New York: Prometheus.

Sternberg, Meir. 1970. "The Compositional Principles of Faulkner's *Light in August* and the Poetics of the Modern Novel." *Hasifrut/Literature* 2:498–537 [Heb.].

———. 1973. "Delicate Balance in the Story of the Rape of Dinah: Biblical Narrative and the Rhetoric of the Narrative Text." *Hasifrut/Literature* 4:193–231 [Heb.].

———. 1974. "What Is Exposition?: An Essay in Temporal Delimination." In *The Theory of the Novel: New Essays,* ed. J. Halperin, 25–70. New York: Oxford Univ. Press.

———. 1978. *Expositional Modes and Temporal Ordering in Fiction.* Baltimore: Johns Hopkins Univ. Press.

———. 1985. *The Poetics of Biblical Narrative: Ideological Literature and the Drama of Reading.* ISBL. Bloomington: Indiana Univ. Press.

———. 1991. "Double Cave, Double Talk: The Indirections of Biblical Dialogue." In *Not in Heaven: Coherence and Complexity in Biblical Narrative,* eds. J. P. Rosenblatt and J. C. Sitterson, 28–57. Bloomington: Indiana Univ. Press.

Talmon, Shemaryahu. 1966. "The 'Desert Motif' in the Bible and in Qumran Literature." In *Biblical Motifs: Origins and Transformations,* ed. A. Altmann, 31–63. Cambridge: Harvard Univ. Press.

Thackeray, H. St. J. and Ralph Marcus, trans. 1977. *Jewish Antiquities, Books 5–8,* by Josephus Flavius. Trans. LCL. Cambridge: Harvard Univ. Press.

Tov, Emanuel. 1992. *Textual Criticism of the Hebrew Bible.* Minneapolis: Fortress Press.

Trible, Phyllis. 1984. *Texts of Terror: Literary-Feminist Readings of Biblical Narratives.* OBT. Philadelphia: Fortress Press.

———. 1991. "Genesis 22: The Sacrifice of Sarah." In *Not in Heaven: Coherence and Complexity in Biblical Narrative,* ed. J. P. Rosenblatt and J. C. Sitterson, 170–91. ISBL. Bloomington: Indiana Univ. Press.

———. 1986. *God and the Rhetoric of Sexuality.* OBT. Minneapolis: Fortress Press.

Tucker, Gene M. 1971. *Form Criticism of the Old Testament.* GBS. Philadelphia: Fortress Press.

Uffenheimer, Benjamin. 1999. *Early Prophecy in Israel.* Trans. D. Louvish. Jerusalem: Magnes Press.

Ulrich, Eugene Charles, Jr. 1978. *The Qumran Text of Samuel and Josephus.* HSM 19. Missoula, Mont.: Scholars Press.

Van Seters, John. 1983. *In Search of History: Historiography in the Ancient World and the Origins of Biblical History*. New Haven: Yale Univ. Press.

Walsh, Jerome T. 1977. "Genesis 2:4b—3:24: A Synchronic Approach." *JBL* 96:161–77.

———. *1 Kings*. 1996. Berit Olam. Collegeville, Minn.: Liturgical.

Weiss, Meir. 1963a. "Einiges über die Bauformen des Erzählens in der Bibel." *VT* 13:456–75.

———. 1963b. "The Poetics of Biblical Narrative: Researching the Biblical Narrative according to the Latest Methods of Literary Criticism." *Molad* 2:402–6.

———. 1965. "Weiteres über die Bauformen des Erzählens in der Bibel." *Bib* 46:181–206.

———. 1983. *The Story of Job's Beginning: Job 1–2, a Literary Analysis*. Trans. R. Rigbi and E. Rigbi. Jerusalem: Magnes Press.

———. 1984 [1962]. *The Bible from Within: The Method of Total Interpretation*. Trans. B. Schwartz. Jerusalem: Magnes Press.

Weitzman, Steven. 1997. *Song and Story in Biblical Narrative: The History of a Literary Convention in Ancient Israel*. ISBL. Bloomington: Indiana Univ. Press.

Wellhausen, Julius. 1957 [1885]. *Prolegomena to the History of Ancient Israel*. Trans. J. S. Black and A. Menzies. New York: Meridian.

Yassif, Eli. 1999. *The Hebrew Folktale: History, Genre, Meaning*. Trans. J. S. Teitelbaum. Folklore Studies in Translation. Bloomington: Indiana Univ. Press.

Zakovitch, Yair. 1982. *The Life of Samson (Judges 13–16): A Critical-Literary Analysis*. Jerusalem: Magnes Press [Heb.].

———. 1984. "The Tale of Naboth's Vineyard: I Kings 21." In Weiss 1984:379–405.

———. 1985. "'Go up, thou bald head; go up, thou bald head': Exegetical Circles in Biblical Narrative." *Jerusalem Studies in Hebrew Literature* 8:7–31.

———. 1990. *Ruth*. Miqra le-Yisrael. Tel Aviv: Am Oved. Jerusalem: Magnes Press [Heb.].

Zeron, Alexander. 1973. "The System of Pseudo-Philo." Ph.D. diss. Tel-Aviv Univ.

Zoran, Gabriel. 1997. *Text, World, Space*. Tel Aviv: Porter Institute for Poetics and Semiotics, Tel Aviv Univ., Hakibbutz Hameuchad [Heb.].

Index of Biblical References